Independent Inquiry into Child Sexual Exploitation in Rotherham 1997 – 2013

The Rotherham Report

August 2014

Rotherham Metropolitan Borough Council

Published by OccupyBawlStreet.com Press (USA)

ISBN-13: 978-0692313565

ISBN-10: 0692313567

Subject Headings:

1. Law Enforcement
2. Failures of leadership
3. Child Protection Service
4. Child Sexual Exploitation
5. Ethnic Origins of Perpetrators
6. Pakistani-Heritage Community
7. Muslim

Independent Inquiry into Child Sexual Exploitation in Rotherham

1997 - 2013

Alexis Jay OBE

Preface

This Independent Inquiry was commissioned by Rotherham Metropolitan Borough Council in October 2013. Its remit, covering the periods of 1997- 2009 and 2009 - 2013, is appended.

The Inquiry applied the definition of child sexual exploitation which is used in Government guidance and is set out in Appendix 4, paragraph 48 of this report. The methodology included reading a wide range of minutes, reports and case files. We also interviewed over a hundred people, either individually or in groups. I agreed with the Chief Executive that the cut-off point for file reading would be the end of September 2013, and that any evidence available to me up till June 2014 would be included in the report. A confidential email and Freepost address was set up. A list of those interviewed is also appended.

At the beginning of the Inquiry, I agreed with the Chief Executive that I would refer to him without delay any instances of individual children where I considered that their circumstances needed urgent attention, or where there was immediate risk. I also agreed to advise him of anything I encountered of a potentially criminal nature, which I would also refer to the Police.

I was assisted in the Inquiry by Kathy Somers, independent consultant and Associate of the Care Inspectorate in Scotland. Specialist expertise was provided by Sheila Taylor and her team at the National Working Group Network on Child Sexual Exploitation, who also carried out cross reading of a small number of files.

Alexis Jay OBE
21 August 2014

Table of Contents

Executive Summary

No one knows the true scale of child sexual exploitation (CSE) in Rotherham over the years. Our conservative estimate is that approximately 1400 children were sexually exploited over the full Inquiry period, from 1997 to 2013.

In just over a third of cases, children affected by sexual exploitation were previously known to services because of child protection and neglect. It is hard to describe the appalling nature of the abuse that child victims suffered. They were raped by multiple perpetrators, trafficked to other towns and cities in the north of England, abducted, beaten, and intimidated. There were examples of children who had been doused in petrol and threatened with being set alight, threatened with guns, made to witness brutally violent rapes and threatened they would be next if they told anyone. Girls as young as 11 were raped by large numbers of male perpetrators.

This abuse is not confined to the past but continues to this day. In May 2014, the caseload of the specialist child sexual exploitation team was 51. More CSE cases were held by other children's social care teams. There were 16 looked after children who were identified by children's social care as being at serious risk of sexual exploitation or having been sexually exploited. In 2013, the Police received 157 reports concerning child sexual exploitation in the Borough.

Over the first twelve years covered by this Inquiry, the collective failures of political and officer leadership were blatant. From the beginning, there was growing evidence that child sexual exploitation was a serious problem in Rotherham. This came from those working in residential care and from youth workers who knew the young people well.

Within social care, the scale and seriousness of the problem was underplayed by senior managers. At an operational level, the Police gave no priority to CSE, regarding many child victims with contempt and failing to act on their abuse as a crime. Further stark evidence came in 2002, 2003 and 2006 with three reports known to the Police and the Council, which could not have been clearer in their description of the situation in Rotherham. The first of these reports was effectively suppressed because some senior officers disbelieved the data it contained. This had led to suggestions of cover-up. The other two reports set out the links between child sexual exploitation and drugs, guns and criminality in the Borough. These reports were ignored and no action was taken to deal with the issues that were identified in them.

In the early 2000s, a small group of professionals from key agencies met and monitored large numbers of children known to be involved in CSE or at risk but their managers gave little help or support to their efforts. Some at a senior level in the Police and children's social care continued to think the extent of the problem, as described by youth workers, was exaggerated, and seemed intent on reducing the official numbers of children categorised as CSE. At an operational level, staff appeared to be overwhelmed by the numbers involved. There were improvements in the response

1

of management from about 2007 onwards. By 2009, the children's social care service was acutely understaffed and over stretched, struggling to cope with demand.

Seminars for elected members and senior officers in 2004-05 presented the abuse in the most explicit terms. After these events, nobody could say 'we didn't know'. In 2005, the present Council Leader chaired a group to take forward the issues, but there is no record of its meetings or conclusions, apart from one minute.

By far the majority of perpetrators were described as 'Asian' by victims, yet throughout the entire period, councillors did not engage directly with the Pakistani-heritage community to discuss how best they could jointly address the issue. Some councillors seemed to think it was a one-off problem, which they hoped would go away. Several staff described their nervousness about identifying the ethnic origins of perpetrators for fear of being thought racist; others remembered clear direction from their managers not to do so.

In December 2009, the Minister of State for Children and Families put the Council's children's safeguarding services into intervention, following an extremely critical Ofsted report. The Council was removed from intervention thirteen months later.

The Rotherham Safeguarding Children Board and its predecessor oversaw the development of good inter-agency policies and procedures applicable to CSE. The weakness in their approach was that members of the Safeguarding Board rarely checked whether these were being implemented or whether they were working. The challenge and scrutiny function of the Safeguarding Board and of the Council itself was lacking over several years at a time when it was most required.

In 2013, the Council Leader, who has held office since 2003, apologised for the quality of the Council's safeguarding services being less than it should have been before 2009. This apology should have been made years earlier, and the issue given the political leadership it needed.

There have been many improvements in the last four years by both the Council and the Police. The Police are now well resourced for CSE and well trained, though prosecutions remain low in number. There is a central team in children's social care which works jointly with the Police and deals with child sexual exploitation. This works well but the team struggles to keep pace with the demands of its workload. The Council is facing particular challenges in dealing with increased financial pressures, which inevitably impact on frontline services. The Safeguarding Board has improved its response to child sexual exploitation and holds agencies to account with better systems for file audits and performance reporting. There are still matters for children's social care to address such as good risk assessment, which is absent from too many cases, and there is not enough long-term support for the child victims.

1. Background

1.1   The Metropolitan Borough of Rotherham is situated in South Yorkshire, about eight miles from Sheffield. The Borough includes Rotherham itself and the outlying towns of Maltby, Rawmarsh, Swinton and Wath on Dearne. More than half of its area is rural. Its population is 258,400. Around 8% of residents are from black and minority ethnic groups. 23% of properties are council rented. Most of the traditional industries from the 19th and 20th centuries have vanished. After a period of decline in the 1980s and '90s, the local economy has grown steadily and the Borough has benefited from inward investment in the fields of technology and light engineering. Nevertheless, there is a wide range of deprivation in the Borough and stark inequalities between some of the areas within it. Unemployment is well above the UK average. The take-up of all welfare benefits is higher than the English average, as are the levels of free school meals and limiting long-term illness.

1.2   The Council comprises 63 elected members, of whom there are 49 Labour, 2 Conservatives, 10 UKIP and 2 Independents. Prior to the local elections in May 2014, there were 57 Labour, 4 Conservatives, 1 UKIP and 1 Independent.

1.3   The earliest reference to sexual exploitation of children reported to the Inquiry was about children in a children's residential unit in the early nineties.

1.4   Until 2004, responsibility for overseeing and coordinating a multi-agency response to child sexual abuse and exploitation lay with the Area Child Protection Committee. In early 2005, this responsibility passed to the Local Safeguarding Children Board (the Safeguarding Board), which was established by the Children Act 2004. Its task is to co-ordinate the actions of agencies represented on the Board and to ensure their effectiveness in safeguarding and promoting the welfare of children in its area.

1.5   In Rotherham, the first Council service to develop a special concern for child sexual exploitation (CSE) was the Risky Business youth project. Founded in 1997, it worked with young people between 11 and 25 years, providing sexual health advice, and help in relation to alcohol and drugs, self-harm, eating disorders, parenting and budgeting. By the late '90s, it was beginning to identify vulnerable girls on the streets of the town. Its relationship with any young person was voluntary on both sides. It was part of the Council's Youth Services, though it derived its funding from various sources in its early years. One of its main functions was the provision of training to voluntary and statutory agencies working in the field, to magistrates, the Police, schools and foster carers.

1.6   Within children's social care[1], the sexual exploitation of young people was first recognised as a Executive Director in 2001, though there were many known cases of CSE in the years before then. Risky Business would refer to children's social care

---

[1] The term 'children's social care' is used throughout the report to refer to the social services provided to children and young people. These had various departmental titles over the years, and are now named Children and Young People's Services.

any young person who gave rise to serious concerns and might require statutory intervention. Between 2001 and 2002, Risky Business participated in a Home Office research pilot whose aim was to find out the most effective approaches to street prostitution. Local agencies challenged the content of the draft report produced in 2002 and questioned its evidence base. While it commended Rotherham's training and fostering programmes, the draft research report contained significant criticisms of the Police and the local authority.

1.7   Social work with the victims of sexual abuse and exploitation had been undertaken largely through the Child Protection Unit and Senior Practitioners. Specialisation became more developed in the early 2000s with the establishment of the Safeguarding Children Unit and the Key Players group. Cases of sexual abuse were managed by qualified social workers under the supervision of their team leaders or locality managers. Strategy meetings were independently chaired by the Safeguarding Children Unit.

1.8   The organisational structure of the Council changed in 2005, with the separation of adult social services from children and families' social services. The new Department of Children and Young People's Services was created.

1.9   In 2003, the Area Child Protection Committee received reports about runaway children and the work of Risky Business. A presentation on sexual exploitation was made to a special seminar for councillors in November 2004. This presentation was explicit about known perpetrators, their ethnic origins, and where they operated. Similar presentations were made to other groups, including the Safeguarding Board, over the following weeks. As a result, the Leader of the Council set up a 'Task and Finish Group' to consider safe travel, safe houses, witness protection, training and publicity to raise public awareness of the issue. Senior councillors attended a conference on child sexual exploitation held in Rotherham in April 2006. A training session for councillors was arranged in June 2007 and a further conference in 2011.

1.10   Around late 2003, the Sexual Exploitation Forum was set up. It was multi-agency and met monthly to consider individual cases of children who were being sexually exploited or at risk of exploitation.

1.11   Between 2007 – 2013, the Police undertook a series of operations, jointly coordinated and designed to investigate cases of suspected child sexual exploitation, although only one resulted in prosecution and convictions. Operation Central in 2008 investigated groups of men believed to be involved in child sexual exploitation. It ended in 2010 with five convictions. In the same year, Child S was murdered. Operation Czar, begun in 2009, led to the issuing of abduction notices, but no convictions. Operation Chard in 2011 led to abduction notices and 11 arrests but no convictions. In the summer of 2012, Operations K-Alphabet and Kappa began, again joint investigations with children's services. Later that year, Operation Carrington investigated the risks to young people in central Rotherham. In 2013, a police operation into historic CSE in Rotherham was announced.

1.12   In October 2012, the Chief Constable gave evidence on child sexual exploitation to the Home Affairs Select Committee.   In January 2013, the Chief Executive and Executive Director for Young People's Services gave evidence. The Select Committee's report was published in June, and was critical of the Council and the Police in Rotherham, particularly for the lack of prosecutions over a number of years.

1.13   In August 2013, the Police and Crime Commissioner announced three reviews of child sexual abuse in the South Yorkshire Police area. In September, the Council announced it would commission this Independent Inquiry.

1.14   A series of audits, reviews, assessments and inspections of the Council's safeguarding and child protection services were conducted over this period.   The Social Services Inspectorate (SSI) and later Ofsted conducted regular inspections, planned or unannounced, notably a full inspection in 2003, a follow-up in 2004, a full inspection in 2008, a 'monitoring visit' in 2009, an unannounced inspection in August 2009, a full inspection in 2010, an unannounced inspection in 2011, and an unannounced review of child protection services in August 2012.   Following the inspection in 2009, the Minister of State for Young People and Families issued to the Council a Notice of Requirement to Improve its children's services. The Notice was removed in January 2011.

1.15   Apart from Ofsted, children's safeguarding services were regularly subject to scrutiny in the form of Joint Area Reviews (JAR), Annual Performance Assessments, periodic thematic audits, and studies by the Council's Scrutiny and Services Improvement Panels.   Serious Case Reviews were undertaken as required.   The Serious Case Review on Child S, whilst judged 'excellent' by Ofsted, was criticised by Michael Gove, former Secretary of State for Education, and by The Times newspaper for the number of redactions the public version contained.

1.16   In 2013 the Leader of the Council formally apologised to the victims of CSE for the response of the Council's safeguarding services for children and young people, up until 2009.

1.17   In addition to the unpublished 2002 Home Office research report, other significant reports relating to the exploitation and abuse of children in Rotherham included two reports by Dr Angie Heal in 2003 and 2006, an external assessment of children's services by Children First (2009), Barnardo's 'Practice Review' (2013), and a 'diagnostic' review by the Chair of the Safeguarding Board (2013).

1.18   From 2003 to the present, articles have appeared in the Times Newspaper critical of the response to child sexual exploitation on the part of South Yorkshire Police and the Rotherham Metropolitan Borough Council.

2. Chronology of key events

A summary of important events in the history of child sexual exploitation in Rotherham.

1997

Risky Business project launched.

1998

December 1998

Draft guidance from the Home Office covering 'Children involved in prostitution'.

1999

January 1999

Communication from South Yorkshire Police giving the policy and procedures for 'the protection of children who are being sexually abused through prostitution'.

February and March 1999

The Social Services (Children and Families) Committee received a report on the Home Office draft guidance. The sub-committee of the Area Child Protection Committee (ACPC) received the draft guidance and the police guidance to officers re 'child sexual exploitation'.

2001

The Council funded Risky Business. Funding was maintained and then increased in 2006.

2002

June 2002

Meetings took place between the Police, the Chief Executive of Rotherham Borough Council and senior staff of Education and Social Services on the subject of the Home Office research report.

December 2002

The ACPC's sub-committee considered a report on 'runaway children' and the protection of children experiencing, or at risk of sexual exploitation.

2003

August 2003

Dr Heal, Strategic Drugs Analyst, produced her first report 'Sexual Exploitation, Drug Use and Drug Dealing: the current situation in South Yorkshire'. The report was circulated to all agencies in the Rotherham Drugs Partnership.

September 2003

The ACPC approved revised procedures and protocols relating to the sexual exploitation of children.

The Sexual Exploitation Forum began its work towards the end of 2003.

2004

November 2004 and early 2005

Presentations on the sexual exploitation of children were made to the Council's Children's Executive Group, the Children and Young People's Board and the Safeguarding Board. It was decided that a Task and Finish Group be set up on this subject, chaired by the Leader of the Council. An Action Plan was called for.

2005

The Task and Finish Group decided to arrange a seminar for all Council members, a Partners Away Day, and major publicity to raise the awareness of the risks of sexual exploitation amongst parents, young people and the community. A group would consider child safety, witness protection, safe travel and issues around licensing and taxis.

April 2005

A seminar for all Council members was organised on the subject of child sexual exploitation. 30 elected members attended. CSE would be a principal theme in the 3-year Community Safety Strategy.

The new department of Children and Young People's Services was created, incorporating previous education functions and children and families' social services. Councillor Shaun Wright was appointed Cabinet Member for Children and Young People's Services.

May 2005

An audit of 87 CSE cases was carried out by the Police on behalf of the Sexual Exploitation Forum.

June 2005

The Forum was dealing with over 90 CSE cases and the decision was taken to reduce the number of cases being discussed.

November 2005

The Chair of the Children and Young People's Voluntary Sector wrote to the Chief Executive, asking how the Task and Finish Group had progressed and offering to contribute to its work. The reply has not been traced.

2006

A conference on the sexual exploitation of children was held in Rotherham in March 2006.

Dr Heal, Strategic Drugs Analyst, produced her second report 'Violence and Gun Crime: Exploitation, Prostitution and Drug Markets in South Yorkshire'. The report was circulated to all agencies in the Rotherham Drugs Partnership.

The funding for Risky Business was increased. The Safeguarding Board approved revised procedures and an 'Action Plan for responding to the sexual exploitation of children and young people in Rotherham'.

August 2006

The Children and Young People's Scrutiny Panel called for an updated report on safeguarding around sexual exploitation.

Three month secondment from National Children's Homes. The secondee began to review referral, assessment, planning etc. relating to the Action Plan. She worked with Risky Business and senior managers of Children and Young People's Services.

2007

January 2007

The Council appointed an Assistant Safeguarding Manager with responsibility for CSE services.

The Director, Targeted Services, took on the management of Risky Business.

April 2007

A Strategic Management Team was established to co-ordinate police and social care input to an investigation of grooming and sexual abuse of young boys. Over 70 alleged victims were identified and an adult male was convicted of offences against

9

10 children. The judge commended the joint work that resulted in the prosecution and conviction of the offender.

June 2007

Shaun Wright, Cabinet Member for Children and Young People's Services, received a report on the 'Protection of Young People from Sexual Assault in Rotherham'. The report was referred to the Children and Young People's Scrutiny Panel and to the Safeguarding Board. It was decided that a training seminar would be held in July for Council members.

December 2007

The Sexual Exploitation Forum heard that Risky Business was inundated with referrals, all of them under 18 years. Some were looked after children. The project was under pressure from those who had referred the children.

2008

Operation Central was set up to investigate men believed to be involved in sexual exploitation. Inter-agency activity was coordinated through the Sexual Exploitation Forum, with input from the Police, Children and Young People's Services and Risky Business. Four young people were witnesses at the subsequent trial, with appropriate support. Five men were subsequently convicted.

Funding for Risky Business was increased.

June 2008

The Safeguarding Board received the annual report on the protection of young people in Rotherham from sexual exploitation. Membership of the Steering Group was expanded to include health and voluntary sector representatives. The 'main service' in this field continued to be Risky Business. It would now promote multi-disciplinary working, group work, a drop-in centre and weekend work.

Work had started involving taxi drivers and licensed premises on the preventive agenda.

July 2008

A new Executive Director of Children and Young People's Services was appointed. Shaun Wright, Cabinet member, received the annual report on the protection of young people in Rotherham from sexual exploitation. He called for a further report on the budget of Risky Business and the likely future pressures on the project. He received a further report on the protection of young people from sexual exploitation in November 2008.

2009

Statutory guidance on safeguarding children and young people from sexual exploitation was received.

January 2009

Shaun Wright, Cabinet member, received a report by the Director of Targeted Services on the progress of arrangements to protect young people from sexual exploitation.

May 2009

An external assessment of Children and Young People's Services, commissioned from Children First, was published.

Autumn 2009

Ofsted rated Rotherham children's services 'inadequate' on the grounds that the safety of children could not be assured. Three areas for priority action were noted.

September 2009

The Local Safeguarding Children Board received a report on the resource implications of the growing demands on the service in relation to sexual exploitation.

October 2009

A new Chief Executive was appointed.

December 2009

The Minister of State served an Improvement Notice on Rotherham Council.

2010

January 2010

Operation Czar began – a joint Police and Children and Young People's Services investigation involving multiple perpetrators and victims. Abduction notices were made, taxi licences were revoked, but no convictions followed.

February 2010

A Lessons Learned review of Operation Central was commissioned.

April 2010

The Safeguarding Board set up the formal Child Sexual Exploitation sub-group.

May 2010

Councillor Paul Lakin became the Lead Member for Children and Young People's Services.

September 2010

The post of specialist CSE Safeguarding Co-coordinator was created and located within the Children's Safeguarding Unit.

November 2010

Operation Central trial ended with five convictions. Child S was murdered, and a Serious Case Review was commissioned by the Safeguarding Board.

December 2010

The support of the Safeguarding Board was sought to the principle of establishing a multi-agency team to address issues of sexual exploitation. The Director of Community Services in Children and Young People's Services emphasised to the Board that the Risky Business service should be further enhanced.

2011

January 2011

Operation Chard began, a joint investigation into multiple perpetrators and victims. Arrests and abduction notices were made, and taxi licences were revoked. One case was referred to the Crown Prosecution Service, but the decision was taken not to proceed.

Rotherham Children's Services were removed from Government intervention.

April 2011

A large regional conference reviewed the lessons learned from Operation Central. The Risky Business project was transferred from Youth Services to Children's Safeguarding Services.

December 2011

A man was convicted and sentenced to 17.5 years for the murder of Child S.

The Safeguarding Board was assured by Council officers that Rotherham was ahead of other areas in its work on the sexual exploitation of young people.

2012

May 2012

The Serious Case Review on Child S was published. The Times newspaper alleged a cover-up on account of the redactions.

July and August 2012

Operation 'K-Alphabet', a joint CSE investigation with Sheffield Police began, focusing on a perpetrator who lived in Rotherham. A second investigation, operation 'Kappa' began. Several other police operations were underway to investigate and prosecute suspected perpetrators.

August 2012

Ofsted rated Rotherham's child protection services as 'adequate' commending 'significant improvements'.

September 2012

The Times reported an alleged cover-up from 1997 to 2010.

The new specialist CSE service was co-located with the Rotherham Police Public Protection Unit with two qualified social workers.

October 2012

The Chief Constable, South Yorkshire Police, attended the Home Affairs Select Committee.

The Overview and Scrutiny Management Board reviewed lessons learned from the Child S Serious Case Review.

November 2012

Operation Carrington began – a joint investigation focusing on Eastern European children who were being sexually exploited/at risk.

2013

January 2013

The Chief Executive and the Executive Director of Children and Young People's Services gave evidence to the Home Affairs Select Committee.

June 2013

The Executive Director of Children and Young People's services advised the Cabinet on the publication of the Home Affairs Select Committee report 'Child Sexual Exploitation and the response to Localised Grooming'. The Cabinet was told that between 2003 and 2009 'we fully acknowledge that our services should have been stronger'.

September 2013

Barnardo's completed a Practice Review, which had been commissioned by Rotherham Borough Council as an initial high-level review of its CSE services.

Councillor Roger Stone, Leader of Rotherham Metropolitan Borough Council, announced that an Independent Inquiry into CSE in Rotherham would be held. He apologised 'unreservedly' to young people who had been let down by the safeguarding services which prior to 2009 'simply weren't good enough'.

Shaun Wright, the Police and Crime Commissioner, announced three reviews of CSE, including an HMIC inspection, an additional team of detectives and other specialists to investigate allegations of historic child abuse in South Yorkshire, and the Chief Crown Prosecutor to review all historic CSE cases across South Yorkshire in which the Crown Prosecution Service was involved. Criminal charges were to be considered.

The incoming Chair of the Local Safeguarding Children Board initiated a 'CSE Diagnostic'.

November 2013

HMIC report on South Yorkshire Police's handling of CSE was published.

December 2013

The Safeguarding Board Chair's 'Diagnostic Report' was published.

3. Inspections and External reviews 1998-2013

Inspections frequently commend the Council for its commitment to safeguarding young people, and its efforts to develop multi-agency responses to child sexual exploitation. However, reports contain serious criticisms, some of which are repeated over the 15-year period. Those that occur most frequently relate to the quality of referrals and assessments, the late provision of reports, the standard of records and reports, and weaknesses in performance management. These included lack of monitoring, inadequate supervision and the absence of sound information systems. The Council was served with an Improvement Notice by the Minister of State for Young People and Families in December 2009, which was lifted in January 2011. In subsequent inspections and reviews, its multi-agency approach to CSE and the specialist team were praised.

3.1   In the first part of this chapter, we summarise the findings of inspections by Ofsted, the Social Services Inspectorate and the Commission for Social Care Inspection. For ease of reference, the findings of reports are described (where possible) under standard headings. We then look at other external reviews which were undertaken between 2009 and 2013.

1998

3.2   The Social Services Inspectorate's report (2003) refers back to the **joint review of social services** in Rotherham held in 1998. The review commended the Council on its realistic strategic plans, its partnership with health, its good relations with users and carers, and its culture of continuous improvement. It called for action in the following areas:

a) Quality of response:

- The standard of assessment and decision-making must be improved

- Information about the supply and demand for services should be carefully analysed

- Agreement should be reached on specific thresholds to achieve the best outcomes for children; and

b) Recording - Standards of recording should be made more consistent.

2003

3.3   **The Social Services Inspectorate (SSI)** conducted an inspection of children's services in February 2003. It found 'a situation of extremes'. It welcomed examples of innovation, moves towards integrated services and new preventive strategies. The Area Child Protection Committee's procedures were up to date. However, core services were under pressure and this was not fully appreciated by the Council. There were serious lapses in initial response, child protection and looked after children systems. Some services were in short supply, compounded by staff vacancy levels.

3.4 Other findings included the following:

a) Quality of Response:

- Referral and assessment teams were responding too slowly and inappropriately to some child protection referrals

- Initial and core assessments were not completed on time. They should draw on information from other agencies and family history

- Child protection conferences were often delayed

- Many reports failed to assess the risks to children and their families

- Urgent action by management was needed to ensure the safety and security of children

- Child protection plans and reviews were variable in quality and lacked a focus on outcomes for the children;

b) Policy and Resources - The Council did not fully appreciate the severe pressures under which core services were operating;

c) Management

- Performance management, information systems and quality assurance arrangements did not identify the lapses which were occurring

- Individual casework and decision-making must be more carefully monitored

- Management information was not routinely used to assess performance as part of a performance management culture

- Monitoring gave too little information about operational performance and the achievement of key targets

- Supervision was not tackling drift in planning and lack of procedural compliance

- The role of senior practitioners was not clear;

d) Training

- Some frontline staff and interviewing officers were not sufficiently skilled to cope with the complexity of referrals

- More staff should attend training in equal opportunities, racial awareness, complaints and customer care;

e) Recording

- The structure of case files should be reviewed to promote effective work with children

- The inspection criticised many aspects of case-recording

- The planning and management of investigations were not recorded as a considered process; and

f) Openness, Equality

- While there were examples of good inter-agency work, the Council was not intervening early enough with other agencies to support families

- There were examples of good work, but more should be done to seek the families' views of services

- Parents were often given insufficient notice of case conferences. Reports were not shared with them

- A racial equality scheme had been published and an Ethnic Minorities Development worker appointed. However, the quality of data on gender and ethnicity was uneven

- Services did not respond consistently to the cultural needs of minority ethnic communities.

3.5 The inspectors had been informed that the Police were often reluctant to engage jointly with the Council in investigations. In one instance, when Police had investigated, the decision that the Crown Prosecution Service would not proceed with criminal charges had taken nine months.

2004

3.6 **The Commission for Social Care Inspection (CSCI)** conducted a follow-up inspection of children's services in June 2004. The report declared that Rotherham was 'heading in the right direction'. Good progress had been made. The positive findings were as follows:

a) Quality of response:

- Responses to referrals were more effective and timely

- Internal audits had improved systems, fewer cases were unallocated and fewer children were on the register

- Assessments and reviews were much improved

- Policies and procedures had been updated

- The front-desk service and the team's new structure were commended; and

b) Management

- Strong senior leadership and an improvement team had been a catalyst for change

- There were plans for more co-located, multi-agency services

- Progress on an integrated agenda would lead to improved services.

3.7 Findings that were more negative included:

a) Policy and Resources

- Office accommodation for frontline staff should be improved

- Children's services needed a higher profile and additional funding to address the agenda of change and development;

b) Management

- Monitoring systems were not 'embedded', so that progress was not maintained

- While more managers were working to a high standard, some middle managers were insufficiently aware of what was happening at the frontline. They had a weak grip on the quality of practice

- The creation of a multi-agency co-located service should be accelerated, together with some restructuring;

c) Training

- Some staff did not understand the new action plan and could not make the changes to practice which were required

- Some staff did not see the need for change and lacked capacity for it. Staff needed training and support to make necessary changes

- Staff needed training in the new computer systems;

d) Recording - The standard of recording should be improved; and

e) Openness, Equality - Along with other agencies, service-users should be better consulted and involved in the development of services.

3.8 There was no mention of the sexual exploitation of children in the follow-up inspection of June 2004, nor in any of the previous inspection reports of which the Inquiry team has a copy.

2005

3.9 **The Annual Performance Assessment** in December 2005 recommended that core assessments be improved and that further efforts be made to agree threshold criteria for children at risk.

2006

3.10 **A Joint Area Review** took place in 2006. The report included a recommendation that the timescales for core assessments be improved. It commended the 'effective systems for sharing information about, and responding to children at risk of domestic violence, sexual exploitation and substance abuse.... through the Risky Business project'. The JAR included the comment that children and young people appeared to be safe from abuse and exploitation. As far as we know, this is the first mention of CSE in an inspection report.

3.11 An inspection report on Rotherham's Youth Services of the same date included a similar finding.

2007/2008

3.12 **The Commission for Social Care Inspection's Annual Performance Reviews** in 2007 and 2008 reported that the Council's record in 'Delivering Outcomes' was 'Good'; its 'Capacity for Improvement' was 'Promising'.

3.13 The reports required that the timescales for the completion of core assessments be improved. They found that management oversight of looked-after children had not ensured that they had been safeguarded.

2009

3.14 **Ofsted** conducted an unannounced inspection of 'contact, referral and assessment arrangements' in August 2009. It found three areas for priority action:

a) Quality of response - The completion of social care assessments was deemed 'particularly weak';

b) Policy and Resources - The wide range of work undertaken by locality social workers undermined their capacity to safeguard vulnerable children; and

c) Management:

- Performance management systems and auditing policies did not ensure that managers could exercise their decision-making and supervisory responsibilities

- Information systems did not provide current and accurate information on contacts, referrals, investigations, assessments and plans.

3.15 These three areas were of sufficient concern that the safety of children could not be assured. In consequence, Rotherham's children's services were rated 'poor'.

3.16 On 16 December 2009, Dawn Primarolo MP, Minister of State for Young People and Families, wrote to the Leader of the Council, serving an **Improvement Notice** on the Council. Improvements were required in the timing, recording and quality of initial and core assessments; in performance management, auditing, scrutiny and quality assurance; in training and staff supervision; in the management of vacancy rates and staff workloads.

2010.

3.17 **Ofsted** conducted an inspection of safeguarding and looked after children in July 2010.

3.18 Safeguarding services were deemed to be 'adequate' in their overall effectiveness and capacity for improvement. The partnership between children's social care, the Police and the voluntary sector was carrying out effective and creative work to prevent sexual exploitation, with cross-agency training.

3.19 The report commended the following initiatives:

a) Policy and Resources:

- The Maltby Linx Young Women's project which worked with those who might be at risk of sexual exploitation

- The Integrated Youth Support service where the lesbian, gay and bisexual group could meet in a safe place and receive support

- The Junction, commissioned by Barnardo's, which was directed towards those who might pose a sexual risk to other young people

- The nursing service which was undertaking joint assessments in children's homes and promoting better understanding of sexual health and relationships; and

b) Management - There was effective, creative multi-agency work to prevent sexual exploitation, coordinated by officers from the Police and social care. Although deemed to be no more than 'adequate', the partnership between children's social care, the Police and voluntary sector monitored children missing from care, from home and school, and was alert to sexual exploitation, bullying and forced marriages.

3.20 **Ofsted** published its Annual Assessment of Rotherham's Children's Services in December 2010. The report acknowledged the work that had been done to bring about the improvements which had been required by previous inspections:

a) Quality of Response - While more initial and full assessments were being carried out on time, the quality of planning and reviews was inadequate, and there was inconsistency in the practice of fieldwork teams;

b) Recording - The quality of recording was inadequate; and

c) Openness, Equality - The inspection of safeguarding had found good examples of involving children in the design of services, but the views of the children were not yet routinely heard at child protection conferences.

2011

3.21 Rotherham's children's services were removed from Government intervention in January 2011.

3.22 **Ofsted** conducted an unannounced inspection of contact, referral and assessment in May 2011.

a) Policy and Resources - The report noted the high level of referrals of domestic violence that were made by the Police to children's social care. This pressure led to delays in screening them;

b) Management

- Quality audits, case monitoring and performance assessment had improved

- The multi-agency partnerships, co-located with social workers, had led to more comprehensive assessments of need and risk

- The regularity and quality of supervision were variable, sometimes poor;

c) Training - Newly qualified social workers did not have access to professional development programmes; and

d) Openness, Equality - The views of young people were more often sought in planning services for them.

3.23 **Ofsted's** Annual Children's Services Assessment took place in November 2011. The Council was commended for having invited a peer challenge team to review its safeguarding services. (The peer challenge review is described later in this chapter). These services were showing improvements. Other comments and recommendations related solely to education services.

2012

3.24 **Ofsted** conducted an inspection of Rotherham's arrangements for the protection of children in July 2012. The findings were:

a) Quality of Response:

- The overall effectiveness of the arrangements to protect children was considered to be 'adequate'

- Information about missing children and children at risk of sexual exploitation was being shared at an early stage and the work was well coordinated

- There was good collaborative work between the local authority and the Police resulting in a targeted approach to tackling sexual exploitation

- The success of this approach was being strengthened by the commitment to create a team of qualified social workers based within the Public Protection Unit

- The inspection called for child-focused risk assessments in cases of domestic abuse and greater challenge of the safeguarding system;

b) Management - With specific reference to the sexual exploitation of children, the report commended the specialist multi-agency team to support children at risk; and

c) Openness, Equality - There should be careful evaluation of the feedback received from children and parents subject to child protection.

3.25 The inspection found that the Local Safeguarding Children Board had become more effective, having established multi-agency sub-groups protecting children at risk of sexual exploitation. A recent serious case review had been considered to be 'excellent' by Ofsted. In order to provide a stronger challenge in key areas of child protection, the Board planned to sharpen its priorities and commission multi-agency case audits.

Other external reviews

3.26   In the rest of this chapter, we summarise the findings of external reviews, together with the review conducted by the Independent Chair of the Safeguarding Board in 2013.

Children First's 'Rotherham Review of Children's Services', 2009

3.27   The Borough Council and NHS Rotherham commissioned Children First to undertake a review of Children and Young People's Services following the negative judgements made in the 2008 Annual Performance Assessment letter. The Assessment had shown deterioration in its overall rating of the services. The sexual exploitation of children was not mentioned either in the Assessment letter or in the Children First Review. In the latter, it was covered by the remit: 'To assess the effectiveness of safeguarding arrangements to ensure that sound and safe practices were in place to protect vulnerable children and young people'.

3.28   The Review commended senior councillors and managers for their commitment to achieving the best outcomes for children and young people, and it endorsed many of the initiatives that the Council and partner agencies had taken in recent years. It recalled the efforts which had been made to achieve truly integrated working with partner agencies around the Change for Children agenda, and concluded that this 'highly ambitious' project had led to a loss of focus on the overall strategic aim and the clarity of its message. It recommended that there be a review of the 'vision, purpose, function and delivery' of services to 'reflect local experience and national expectations'.

3.29   In commending the current Action Plan, the Review drew attention to the 'excessive number of teams and panels', which could lead to confusion and increased risk. There was confusion about line management and accountability for outcomes; self-evaluation and quality assurance lacked rigour and effective challenge; information was not adequately monitored or used for performance improvement.

3.30   While supporting the move towards an integrated model of services, the Review thought that the Borough could do more. Staff should be fully trained to understand the model's implications; procedures should be directed towards its effective application; the relationship between central services and locality teams was confused and should be clarified.

3.31   The Review expressed concern that children's social care in Rotherham was inadequately funded, not least its high-risk services. The very high rate of referrals reflected the social conditions in many parts of the Borough, the chronic neglect, the poor standards of child care, the level of domestic violence and drug abuse, all of which had a direct impact on the welfare and safety of children.

3.32   The report was commissioned by the Local Safeguarding Children Board in April 2010 and submitted at the end of July 2010. It was carried out by Malcolm Stevens, Justice Care Solutions. Its aim was to examine how individuals and agencies worked together on CSE, and to make recommendations with a view to improving liaison and identifying lessons to be learned.

3.33   Operation 'Central' investigated alleged CSE offences committed against many girls by males aged 20-29. Charges were brought in respect of four girls aged 12-16. At the time of the review, a criminal trial was underway at the Crown Court, hence there were some limitations on the evidence that could be used in the report. The defendants were eight local men of Asian origin. Five were convicted.

3.34   The evidence suggested that CSE in Rotherham was extremely serious. The report praised the Safeguarding Board for seeking to 'identify, adapt, adopt and improve'. The report relied on transcripts of interviews by the Police with victims, scrutiny of inspections, reports and other records.

3.35   The Police were said in the review to have shown patience, care and empathy in helping the girls relate their stories. The report described the grooming techniques used towards the girls. It was clear that the offences under Operation Central represented a small proportion of current CSE offences in the Borough. Any connection between the offences and illicit substance abuse was said to be peripheral and tenuous. There appeared to be no link with prostitution. Apart from the gift of a mobile phone, victims received no reward or inducement. The report deplored the BNP's campaign based on the Asian origin of the perpetrators.

3.36   Emma Jackson, a survivor, said that few practitioners understood what went on. Risky Business was helpful and trustworthy.

> "They didn't listen to me...they must be trained to understand CSE better and intervene earlier. There should be more people like Risky Business".

3.37   The review looked at one case ('Child 3') in detail. Findings included:

   a) Information from the school, social care, police and the youth service was not submitted to the Strategy meetings;

   b) key indicators were missed;

   c) Strategy meetings' recommendations were not acted upon;

   d) the Youth Offending Team was always absent from Strategy meetings;

   e) social care was inadequately represented; failings in consistency and seniority of attendance;

   f) follow-up meetings were cancelled or postponed; too little priority was given to the CSE concerns of Risky Business and the police PPU;

g) agencies did not know which others, if any, were involved in a case;

h) Child 3 was treated as a criminal; and

i) there was 'over reliance on Strategy meetings rather than effective case management at locality level'.

3.38 Risky Business was well thought of by young people. It was helpful to the Police. It attended all Strategy meetings and had good working relations with the PPU and Safer Neighbourhood Teams. Its location was unsuitable and its specialist computer systems were not operational. The police PPU was well integrated within the CSE networks and worked well with Risky Business and social care teams.

3.39 The report sought a greater role for Risky Business in 'ensuring that whatever actions were necessary were actioned in a way acceptable to victims'. A multi-agency team should be built around Risky Business to specialise in tackling CSE (prevention, protection, disruption, training, support, supervision). Still in the context of Risky Business and the CSE team, the report talked of better co-ordination, management, monitoring and intelligence, but this was 'not a recommendation for more resources'. It even suggested that Risky Business should 'pursue, support and co-ordinate children's entitlement to compensation'.

3.40 In addition to the above, the report sought better support for, and protection of witnesses at the Crown Court. Other recommendations related to:

a) Victims' wishes to be obtained throughout the trial and afterwards;

b) Likewise, parents' views should be obtained;

c) The function and conduct of Strategy meetings to be reviewed;

d) The Youth Offending Team should be more involved in CSE proceedings; and

e) Staff working directly with CSE cases to be offered counselling.

The Safeguarding Peer Challenge, 2011

3.41 This was organised by the Local Government Association in November 2011. Its findings were:

a) Quality of Response - On safeguarding services, it called for a stronger focus on outcomes for children, on the effectiveness of the services in making a difference to children's lives;

b) Management:

- The report commended strong political and managerial leadership

- Roles and responsibilities of the several Boards and Partnerships should be clarified and their plans and expectations made more widely known;

c) Openness and Equality – The report commended:

- the level of partnership and joint working with the voluntary sector

- a commitment to user engagement and the safeguarding of children.

Barnardo's 'Rotherham Practice Review report', October 2013

3.42   In August 2013, Rotherham Metropolitan Borough Council commissioned Barnardo's to undertake an 'initial high-level review' of CSE services. The review covered the effectiveness of inter-agency working; the current model of service delivery; the training strategy; the sharing of information and the multi-agency risk assessment model. The report commended agencies and Council members for their commitment to addressing CSE and their plans to widen the inter-agency partnership to include businesses, social landlords and local communities. It suggested further extension of the partnership to include hotels and B&Bs, taxis and public transport, food outlets, shopping centres, pubs and clubs.

3.43   The report drew attention to the severe pressures under which the CSE specialist team was working. The team was still in the development phase. A named, designated manager should be made responsible for the day-to-day work of the team. Senior managers were making heavy demands relating to performance management and data-collection, some of which did not relate to CSE. Management of the team was made more difficult by the differing priorities of its constituent members. At all levels, staff were feeling over-managed. There was additional anxiety arising from recent media interest, the Home Affairs Select Committee and the threat of inspection.

3.44   Further progress was recommended in the integration and training of professionals in the identification and prevention of CSE, within the overall embrace of the Safeguarding Board. Multi-agency working called for the removal of barriers that were based on stereotypical viewpoints of police, health and social care. Engagement with young people and their families required a different approach from traditional policing and social work methods, and different operational processes.

3.45   The report noted that an inter-agency communications strategy was being devised. It called for further improvements in the analysis of information relating to the victim, the offender and the location; and for staff training to ensure that the system worked effectively. The outreach work should be expanded to become more clearly targeted, more assertive, and more directed towards early intervention. The report listed the services in health and education that should contribute to this process. Through a 'train the trainer' approach, training should be extended to all faith groups and communities including the business community.

Rotherham Local Safeguarding Children Board 'Review of the response to child sexual exploitation in Rotherham' December 2013

3.46   This report was compiled at the initiative of Steve Ashley who took up his appointment as Independent Chair of the Board in September of that year. He was assisted in the study by a small group of independent persons with wide experience in this field. The terms of reference were to review the way in which members of the Safeguarding Board co-operate together and contribute to the Board's work; the effectiveness of their current plans; and the benchmarking of Rotherham's services against national standards. The terms included the provision of proposals for the governance of the Safeguarding Board in relation to child sexual exploitation (CSE) and a review of progress made against the recommendations of earlier inspections and reports.

3.47   The review gave an overview of the current arrangements. It was sensitive to the great pressures to which the Borough Council had been subject in recent months and the effect which these pressures had upon staff at all levels. It recognised the efforts that had been made since 2010 to improve the response that the Council and its partner agencies had made towards child sexual exploitation. It recorded the determination that staff were showing towards the attainment of excellence in this difficult work.

3.48   The report understood the reasons for the creation of a specialist multi-agency team dealing with CSE, and it suggested that the team should, in time, become integrated within the mainstream of children's services.

3.49   The review put forward cogent arguments for the improved management of the multi-agency CSE team. As the paper suggested, the CSE team had been set up in a hurry at a time of considerable turmoil. A new management structure would strengthen accountability and remove the ambiguities that existed in the present arrangements.

3.50   The review team considered the governance structures to be difficult to understand. This lack of comprehension extended to staff at all levels. The team also found confusion about the roles and responsibilities of the several bodies functioning within the system. There was a risk of overlap between the various groups and sub-groups, leading to blurred accountability. The membership of some could be reduced with profit.

3.51   The current action plan was deemed to be too complicated and lacking a clear focus on outcomes for children. It should be a more workable document setting priorities that were truly achievable. Again many staff did not appear to understand the plan or its significance. Although the review did not state this explicitly, it implied that preparation of the plan had been absorbing a disproportionate amount of management time, more of which should have been devoted to ensuring high quality work with children and families at the one-to-one level.

3.52   The review supported the absorption of Risky Business into the multi-disciplinary safeguarding structure. It talked of Risky Business as having 'failed' because of the weight of expectations placed upon it. It recommended that the CSE team should forge closer links with the Integrated Youth and Support Service (IYSS) to ensure that the 'Prevent' approach to the work be maintained and developed.

HMIC independent Assessment of South Yorkshire Police's Response to Child Sexual Exploitation, 2013

3.53 In August 2013, the Police and Crime Commissioner (PCC) for South Yorkshire Police asked Her Majesty's Inspectorate of Constabulary to provide an independent assessment of the arrangements made by South Yorkshire Police to protect children from sexual exploitation, and to make recommendations. The report dealt with issues of leadership, strategies, structures, processes, training, intelligence and innovation. It identified strengths and weaknesses under each heading, and listed actions to be undertaken in the short, medium and longer terms.

3.54 The report found all staff to be 'conscientious, enthusiastic and focused on providing good outcomes for the children with whom they work'. More staff had been dedicated to CSE. The force had improved its engagement with other agencies working in this field and had co-operated with them in developing strategies for preventing children becoming victims of CSE; for protecting those at risk; and for supporting children in all situations. It had done good work in schools, particularly in relation to internet safety. All 1700 frontline staff had received training in CSE work. The report commended South Yorkshire Police's comprehensive action on the sexual exploitation of children.

3.55 The PCC and the Chief Constable had stated that the protection of children from sexual exploitation was a top priority for the force. The report found, however, that this had not been translated into operational activity on the ground at local level. Local resources were not fully supporting investigations of CSE. Many staff felt that senior and middle managers were more focused on dealing with offences such as burglary and vehicle crime. Since there were no operational targets for dealing with CSE, it lost out to crimes that were governed by them. Many officers and staff were confused about the messages that they received from senior leaders about CSE, to the extent that they did not know who had overall responsibility for this aspect of their work. Staff in the Public Protection and CSE units were working in crowded offices; they were ill equipped and were struggling to manage their caseloads. In Rotherham, these caseloads were deemed to be especially hard to manage.

3.56 The report called on South Yorkshire Police to improve the auditing and recording of its response to CSE; to evaluate the effect of the changes which it was making, especially in relation to its protective work; and to apply research and analysis to support police work on CSE, together with improved monitoring of the internet for evidence of it.

4. The scale of child sexual exploitation in Rotherham

No one knows the true scale of sexual exploitation in Rotherham over the years. Our conservative estimate is that there were more than 1400 victims in the period covered by the Inquiry, and an unknown number who were at risk of being exploited. Child victims of sexual exploitation make up a tiny proportion of contacts and referrals to children's social care, but they constitute a very significant proportion of the children at risk of serious injury and harm. Even in 2014, young people told us they would be reluctant to come forward for help because they would feel ashamed or afraid. Many more females than males have been identified as having been sexually exploited, and there must be concern about under-reporting of exploitation of young males. Some children are exposed to exploitation when they become looked after. And some exploited children are used by perpetrators to gain access to looked after children. It is a matter of particular concern when children are placed out of their home area. This is a cross boundary issue that requires clear agreements between Councils in the interest of safeguarding all looked after children.

The Scale of the Problem in Rotherham

4.1 Children's social care introduced CSE as a category for referral in 2001. However, many exploited children were wrongly categorised as being 'out of control'. Prior to January 2013, the Police did not have a separate category for CSE. Neither agency had compiled reliable data that the Inquiry could use to estimate the scale of the problem over time. There was good information about cases open to the CSE team or co-worked by them, but information about other children being supported by children's social care was not easily obtained.

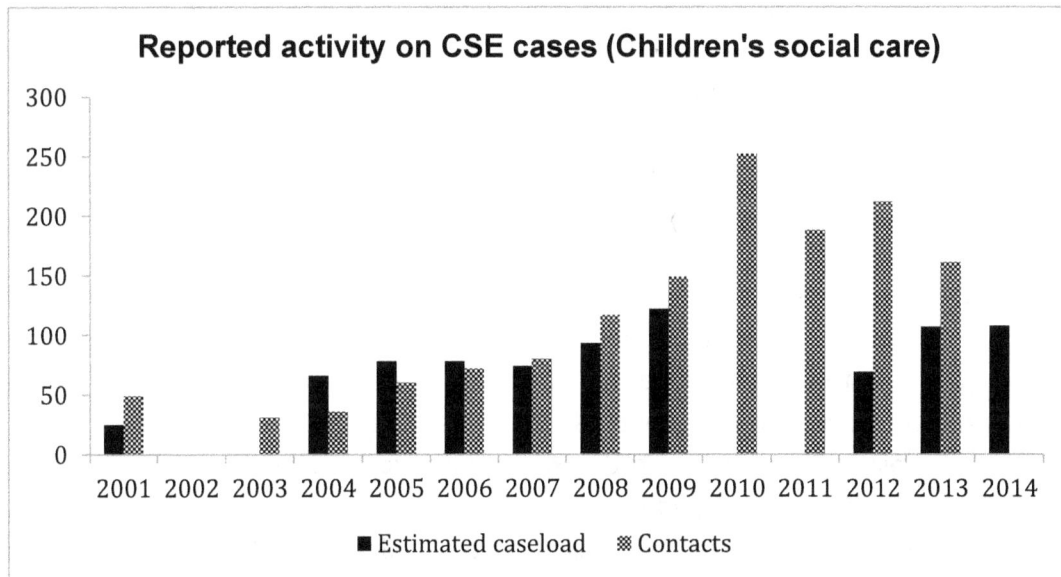

Reported activity on CSE cases (Children's social care)

4.2 In the chart above we summarise what we were able to find out about caseloads and contacts received by children's social care. The data must be treated with caution. The figures were not collected or presented in a systematic way from year to year. Nevertheless, the chart gives a broad indication of the scale of the problem as reflected in children's social care records.

4.3 The Inquiry was given a list of 988 children known to children's social care, or the Police. 51 were current cases and 937 historic. We read 66 case files in total.

4.4 We took a randomised sample of 19 current and 19 historic cases. In 95% of the files sampled, there was clear evidence that the child had been a victim of sexual exploitation. Only two children (5%) were at risk of being exploited rather than victims. From the random samples, we concluded that it was very probable that a high proportion of the 988 children were victims.

4.5 A further 28 case files were read. 22 were historic cases sampled from lists of suspected victims in police operations, including Central, Czar and Chard. Three were current cases brought to our attention during the course of the Inquiry, and three were historic cases of children who had been highlighted by national media. All 28 children were victims of sexual exploitation.

4.6 To help reach an overall estimate of the problem, we used reports to the Local Safeguarding Children Board (formerly the ACPC) and Council committees. We examined minutes of the Sexual Exploitation Forum and minutes of independently chaired Strategy meetings where individual children were discussed. These included inter-agency discussions about hundreds of children who had suffered, or were at serious risk of sexual exploitation. We also had access to lists, and sometimes summary descriptions, of many hundreds of children who were supported by Risky Business, individually or in group sessions.

4.7 Taking all these sources together, the Inquiry concluded that at least 1400 children were sexually exploited between 1997 and 2013. This is likely to be a conservative estimate of the true scale of the problem. We are unable to assess the numbers of other children who may have been at risk of exploitation, or those who were exploited but not known to any agency. This includes some who were forced to witness other children being assaulted and abused.

4.8 During the Inquiry, senior managers in children's social care commented to us that CSE comprises a very small proportion of the total contacts/referrals to children's social care – just over 2%. One manager was reported in a recent minute of the Child Sexual Exploitation sub-group as saying that 'agencies need to retain a sense of proportionality with regard to child sexual exploitation, as it only actually accounts for 2.3% of the Council's safeguarding work in Rotherham. Although it is a very important issue, child neglect is a much more significant problem'. This is not an appropriate message for senior managers to give. We fully support the view expressed by police officers responsible for CSE in Rotherham – 'It may be 2% of referrals but these children are a high proportion of the children most at risk of serious injury and harm'.

4.9 In 2013, South Yorkshire Police received 157 reports concerning child sexual exploitation in Rotherham. Police activity[2] since 2012 was as follows:

	Prosecutions	Cautions	No further action (CPS)[3]	No further action (D.I)[4]	Abduction Notices
2012	8	0	0	2	7
2013	9	2	0	7	17
2014[5]	1	0	0	0	6

4.10   Child sexual exploitation became the focus of attention in Rotherham in the late 1990s, when the Risky Business project was established. Several experienced workers told us that they had come across examples of child sexual exploitation from the early – mid 1990s onward, and there was awareness at that time that looked after children in local residential units were at risk of being targeted.

4.11   At the time of the Inquiry there was no standardised reporting of child sexual exploitation that would allow reliable judgements about whether child sexual exploitation was more or less prevalent in Rotherham than in other parts of the country and the very nature of the problem means that accurate reporting will continue to be a challenge. It seems likely that the existence of the Risky Business project, its ability to attract referrals directly from children and parents affected by sexual exploitation, and the attention given to child sexual exploitation at a multi-agency level over the years meant that the problem would have been more visible in Rotherham than in some other parts of the country.

4.12   Many of the young people we met knew victims of CSE, either family members or young people they knew from school. They gave examples of children being bullied and ostracised at school because they were involved in sexual exploitation, and also knew children who became looked after and were placed far away from Rotherham. They told us that children would be reluctant to seek help because they would be ashamed and also afraid that they would be placed out of the area far away from their families and friends. One young person told us that 'gang rape' was a usual part of growing up in the area of Rotherham in which she lived.

Risk Factors

4.13   Risk factors for CSE are increasingly well understood. The majority of children whose files we read had multiple reported missing episodes. Addiction and mental health emerged as common themes in the files. Almost 50% of children who were sexually exploited or at risk had misused alcohol or other substances (this was typically part of

---

[2] The figures do not include offences against Rotherham children who were trafficked to other areas; these are recorded in the area where the offence took place
[3] Decision taken by Crown Prosecution Service
[4] Decision taken by Detective Inspector, South Yorkshire Police
[5] 2014 figures are for Quarter 1 only.

the grooming process), a third had mental health problems (again, often as a result of abuse) and two thirds had emotional health difficulties. There were issues of parental addiction in 20% of cases and parental mental health issues in over a third of cases. Barriers to accessing specialist counselling and/or mental health services for children and young people were a recurrent theme. This was a feature in current as well as historic cases.

4.14 In just over a third of cases, children affected by sexual exploitation were previously known to services because of child protection and child neglect. There was a history of domestic violence in 46% of cases. Truancy and school refusal were recorded in 63% of cases and 63% of children had been reported missing more than once.

4.15 We cover looked after children in Chapter 6.

Gender

4.16 Generally, there has been relatively low reporting of sexual exploitation of young males, with the exception of the police operation and a criminal conviction in 2007 of an offender who abused over 80 boys and young men. Over the years, this was identified at inter-agency meetings and in CSE plans as an issue that required attention in Rotherham. That continues to be the case today.

4.17 Six of the CSE team's caseload at May 2014 were male, and 45 female.

4.18 We read the files of ten boys who were groomed and abused by the lone male prosecuted and sentenced in 2007, and a further seven files of boys/young men who were his alleged victims. Following the trial, children's social care considered only two of the ten victims to meet the threshold for social care, although many had been raped and at least one was suspected of being involved in abusing other child victims. So far as we could ascertain from the files, none of these children was referred to Risky Business, and only one was referred for specialist counselling, where there was a long waiting list. One of the children who failed to meet the threshold for social care went on to become a serious sex offender, convicted of the abduction and rape of young girls.

4.19 The Inquiry team did a detailed analysis of four cases involving young boys. We reviewed one young teenager with the specialist team from the National Working Group Network. Several issues emerged from the latter case, including:

a) the importance of making sure that judgments about child sexual exploitation are consistent and gender neutral, for example by asking if the same level of risk would be acceptable if the child was the opposite gender;

b) supporting children to explore their sexuality in safe ways, including building links and referral pathways to local LGBT projects that could provide appropriate information and advice; and

c) understanding the extreme danger children could put themselves in when they made contact with predatory adults because they did not know where else to find out about their sexuality. This needed to be better reflected in risk assessments.

5. The children who were victims of sexual exploitation.

The impact of sexual exploitation on the lives of young victims has been absolutely devastating, not just when they were being abused, but for many years afterwards. Here we describe how the lives of these children were affected by the trauma they suffered.

5.1   The primary source of evidence for this chapter derives from 66 case files read by the Inquiry team. This was checked against minuted case discussions, letters from and interviews with parents, and a small number of interviews with young people who had been sexually exploited.

5.2   Meetings of the Sexual Exploitation Forum discussed individual children, as did independently chaired case conferences and Strategy meetings. Their minutes were often detailed, and covered many hundreds of children, and a significant number of suspected perpetrators. These were inter-agency meetings where information and assessments were validated or contested by professionals from the different organisations. The Inquiry team has also checked its evidence against the findings in other reports, notably those in the 'Home Office report' summarised in chapter 10. No contrary evidence was found in any of these sources.

5.3   The Inquiry team concluded that the case files and the other sources described above contained accurate information about the experiences of the child victims.

5.4   The cases described in this chapter are very typical of many of the files we read and were chosen to give a fair reflection of what many victims experienced. They include some, but by no means all, of the most serious cases we read. All of the children described in this section were under the age of 16 when they were first abused. Every effort has been made to protect the identity of the victims and minor details have been omitted or altered where necessary. Quotes throughout this chapter are taken directly from what children and their parents said or wrote.

5.5   In this part of the report, we have not specified the ethnicity of the victims or the perpetrators. In a large number of the historic cases in particular, most of the victims in the cases we sampled were white British children, and the majority of the perpetrators were from minority ethnic communities. They were described generically in the files as 'Asian males' without precise reference being made to their ethnicity.

Experiences of Exploited Children

5.6   It is difficult to describe the appalling nature of the abuse that the victims of sexual exploitation in Rotherham have endured over the years. Victims were raped by multiple perpetrators, trafficked to other towns and cities in the North of England,

5.7   abducted, beaten and intimidated. Some of their experiences were described in national media reports. We read three case files that had been covered by the media, and considered the reporting to be accurate.

5.8 We read cases where a child was doused in petrol and threatened with being set alight, children who were threatened with guns, children who witnessed brutally violent rapes and were threatened that they would be the next victim if they told anyone. Girls as young as 11 were raped by large numbers of male perpetrators, one after the other.

"What's the point… I might as well be dead."

5.9 In two of the cases we read, fathers tracked down their daughters and tried to remove them from houses where they were being abused, only to be arrested themselves when police were called to the scene. In a small number of cases (which have already received media attention) the victims were arrested for offences such as breach of the peace or being drunk and disorderly, with no action taken against the perpetrators of rape and sexual assault against children.

5.10 There are numerous historic examples (up to the mid-2000s) of children being stalked by their abusers, and some extreme cases of violent threats or actual assaults on the victims and their families.

5.11 One parent, who agreed to her child being placed in a residential unit in order to protect her, wrote to children's social care expressing her fears for her daughter's safety. She described her despair that instead of being protected, her child was being exposed to even worse abuse than when she was at home:

"My child (age 13) may appear to be a mature child, yet some of her actions and the risks to which she constantly puts herself are those of a very immature and naïve person. She constantly stays out all night getting drunk, mixing with older mature adults, and refuses to be bound by any rules."

5.12 One child who was being prepared to give evidence received a text saying the perpetrator had her younger sister and the choice of what happened next was up to her. She withdrew her statements. At least two other families were terrorised by groups of perpetrators, sitting in cars outside the family home, smashing windows, making abusive and threatening phone calls. On some occasions child victims went back to perpetrators in the belief that this was the only way their parents and other children in the family would be safe. In the most extreme cases, no one in the family believed that the authorities could protect them.

5.13 Many of the victims were unable to recognise that they had been groomed and exploited, and some blamed themselves not just for their own abuse, but for what happened to other victims.

5.14 There have been a small number of successful prosecutions for offences against individual children. The courage required of children to give evidence against their attackers has been rightly commended, but the challenges cannot be underestimated. Many other children refused to give evidence and/or withdrew statements as a direct result of threats, intimidation and assaults against them or their families. Overall, the small number of prosecutions and convictions has been disproportionate to the numbers of children abused and the seriousness of the offences committed against them.

Grooming

5.15 The process of grooming has been well documented in national reports and research. Many of the cases we examined showed classic evidence of grooming. Many of the children were already vulnerable when grooming began. The perpetrators targeted children's residential units and residential services for care leavers. It was not unusual for children in residential services and schools to introduce other children to the perpetrators.

> *"I know he really loves me … (about a perpetrator convicted of very serious offences against other children)"*

5.16 Many of the case files we read described children who had troubled family backgrounds, with a history of domestic violence, parental addiction, and in some cases serious mental health problems. A significant number of the victims had a history of child neglect and/or sexual abuse when they were younger. Some had a desperate need for attention and affection.

> *"He may have other girlfriends but I am special…"*

5.17 Schools raised the alert over the years about children as young as 11, 12 and 13 being picked up outside schools by cars and taxis, given presents and mobile phones and taken to meet large numbers of unknown males in Rotherham, other local towns and cities, and further afield. Typically, children were courted by a young man whom they believed to be their boyfriend. Over a period of time, the child would be introduced to older men who cultivated them and supplied them with gifts, free alcohol and sometimes drugs. Children were initially flattered by the attention paid to them, and impressed by the apparent wealth and sophistication of those grooming them.

> *"Boys gave me drink and drugs for free… I was driven around in fast cars".*

5.18 Many were utterly convinced that they were special in the affections of a perpetrator, despite all the evidence that many other children were being groomed and abused by the same person. Some of the victims were never able to accept that they had been groomed and abused by one or more sexual predators. A key objective of the perpetrators was to isolate victims from family and friends as part of the grooming process.

5.19 Over time, methods of grooming have changed as mobile technology has advanced.

Mobile phones, social networking sites and mobile apps have become common ways of identifying and targeting vulnerable children and young people and we heard concerns from local agencies in Rotherham that much younger children were being targeted in this way. A number of the recent case files we read demonstrated that by unguarded use of text and video messaging and social networking sites, children had unwittingly placed themselves in a position where they could be targeted, sometimes in a matter of days or hours, by sexual predators from all over the world. In a small number of cases, this led to direct physical contact, rape and sexual abuse with one or more perpetrators. The comment was made that grooming could move from online to personal contact very quickly indeed. One of the most worrying features is the ease with which young children aged from about 8-10 years can be targeted and exploited in this way without their families being aware of the dangers associated with internet use.

5.20 Several social work practitioners told us that they were aware of the problem of the sexual exploitation of children in Rotherham from the early to mid-1990s, although it was not well recognised or understood and was often described as 'child prostitution'. By the late 1990s, Rotherham was one of a relatively small number of places where the problem was being addressed. In 2000, Risky Business delivered training on the sexual exploitation of children to many local agencies, and there was a growing awareness of the seriousness of the problem locally and the numbers of children and young people affected.

5.21 **Child A (2000)**[6] was 12 when the risk of sexual exploitation became known. She was associating with a group of older Asian men and possibly taking drugs. She disclosed having had intercourse with 5 adults. Two of the adults received police cautions after admitting to the Police that they had intercourse with Child A. Child A continued to go missing and was at high risk of sexual exploitation. A child protection case conference was held. It was agreed by all at the conference that Child A should be registered. However, the CID representative argued against the category of sexual abuse being used because he thought that Child A had been '100% consensual in every incident'. This was overruled, with all others at the case conference demonstrating a clear understanding that this was a crime and a young child was not capable of consenting to the abuse she had suffered. She was supported appropriately once she was placed on the child protection register.

5.22 **Child B (2001)** was referred to Risky Business by her school when she was 15 years old. By that time, she had been groomed by an older man involved in the exploitation of other children. Child B loved this man and believed he loved her. He trafficked her to Leeds, Bradford and Sheffield and offered to provide her with a flat in one of those cities. A child protection referral was made but the social care case file recorded no response to this. The case was discussed at regular Key Players

---

[6] The year in brackets is the year is when sexual exploitation is first known to have occurred, or when the risk of exploitation was identified.

meetings (no records of these meetings have survived). Within just a few months, Child B and her family were living in fear of their lives. The windows in their house were put in. She and her family received threats that she would be forced into prostitution. Child B was assaulted by other victims at the instigation of the perpetrator. An attack on her older sibling by associates of the perpetrator resulted in him being hospitalised with serious injuries. Child B also required hospital treatment for injuries she sustained. A younger child in the family was threatened and had to go into hiding so that the perpetrators could not carry out threats against her. Child B and her mother refused to have anything more to do with the Police, because they believed the Police could do nothing to protect them. Child B had been stalked and had petrol poured over her and was threatened with being set alight. She took overdoses. She and her family were too terrified to make statements to the Police. By the time Child B was 18, her family situation had broken down and she was homeless. She referred herself to children's social care, and was given advice about benefits. No further action was taken. This child and her family were completely failed by all services with the exception of Risky Business.

5.23 **Child C (2002)** was 14 when sexual exploitation was identified. She was referred several times to children's social care between 2002 and 2004 because of family breakdown. She was described as being out of control. Her mother voiced her concerns about Child C being sexually active, going missing and repeated incidents of severe intoxication when she had been plied with drink by older males. Several initial assessments were carried out and some family support was offered. The case was then closed. The social worker's assessment was that Child C's mother was not able to accept her growing up. In fact, she was displaying what are now known to be classic indicators of child sexual exploitation from the age of 11. By the age of 13, she was at risk from violent perpetrators, associating with other victims of sexual exploitation, misusing drugs, and at high risk. She was referred to Risky Business whose staff identified these risk factors and addressed them through a planned programme of preventive work.

5.24 **Child D (2003)** was 13 when she was groomed by a violent sexual predator who raped and trafficked her. Her parents, Risky Business and Child D herself all understood the seriousness of the abuse, violence and intimidation she suffered. Police and children's social care were ineffective and seemed to blame the child. A core assessment was done but could not be traced on the file. An initial assessment accurately described the risks to Child D but appeared to blame her for 'placing herself at risk of sexual exploitation and danger'. Other than Risky Business, agencies showed no comprehension that she had been groomed at 13, that she was terrified of the perpetrators, and that her attempts to placate them were themselves a symptom of the serious emotional harm that CSE had caused her. Risky Business worked very hard with Child D and her parents. None of the other agencies intervened effectively to protect her, and she and her parents understandably had no confidence in them.

5.25 **Child E (2004)** became a looked after child when she was aged 12. She had an abusive family background and her parents had mental health problems. She became a victim of child sexual exploitation while she was looked after in a local children's unit. Her looked after file could not be traced, although minutes from looked after reviews were accessed on the Risky Business file. Child E was described as very naïve, and desperate for affection. She was very vulnerable to coercion and was sexually exploited when a looked after child by adult males she thought were her boyfriends. Notes from the children's unit files at the time suggest there was a level of chaos surrounding the care of Child E and other children in the unit, with staff powerless as older children in the residential units introduced younger and more vulnerable children like Child E to predatory adult males who were targeting children's homes.

5.26 Whilst looked after, she was prematurely moved into semi-independent accommodation, where she became even more at risk of harm. She was then admitted to a residential adolescent mental health unit after she suffered a psychotic episode. There is evidence on the file that at that point every effort was made by social care staff to support her and find a suitable care placement. She was found a specialist foster placement at the age of 16, and benefited from a supportive and caring environment. Whilst there was some evidence of positive outcomes when she was 16, the longer term outcomes for this child are not known.

5.27 **Child F (2006)** was a victim of serious sexual abuse when she was a young child. She was groomed for sexual exploitation by a 27-year-old male when she was 13. She was subjected to repeated rapes and sexual assaults by different perpetrators, none of whom were brought to justice. She repeatedly threatened to kill herself and numerous instances of serious self-harm were recorded in the case file, including serious overdoses and trying to throw herself in front of cars. Social workers worked to protect Child F after she was referred by the Police. There was good cooperation between children's social care services, the Police, Risky Business and acute hospital services, where doctors were seriously concerned about her because of the number and seriousness of hospital admissions over such a short time, many associated with serious drug misuse and self-harm. There was evidence in the file of social workers, frontline managers and Risky Business workers doing everything possible to help Child F. She was eventually placed in secure care, where she stayed for several months. During this time she was kept safe and a process of therapeutic intervention began.

5.28 Child F was supported to return home, but because her family moved out of the area, we do not know what the outcomes were for her.

5.29 **Child G (2007)** went missing twice in quick succession when she was 14. Referrals were made by the Police to children's social care but these were not followed up. She was then groomed and raped by a predatory male who was later convicted and sentenced. There was serious concern that she was at risk of suicide around the time of her rape and the subsequent court case. The case was kept open during criminal proceedings, but closed thereafter with no record of the outcomes for Child G, who was then 16 years old.

5.30 **Child H (2008)** was 11 years old when she came to the attention of the Police. She disclosed that she and another child had been sexually assaulted by adult males. When she was 12, she was found drunk in the back of a car with a suspected CSE perpetrator, who had indecent photos of her on his phone. Risky Business became involved and the Locality Team did an initial assessment and closed the case. Her father provided Risky Business with all the information he had been able to obtain about the details of how and where his daughter had been exploited and abused, and who the perpetrators were. This information was passed on to the authorities. Around this time, there were further concerns about her being a victim of sexual exploitation. She was identified as one of a group of nine children associating with a suspected CSE perpetrator. Her case had not been allocated by children's social care. The Chair of the Strategy meeting expressed concern about her and considered she needed a child protection case conference. This does not appear to have been held. Three months later, the social care manager recorded on the file that Child H had been assessed as at no risk of sexual exploitation, and the case was closed. Less than a month later, she was found in a derelict house with another child, and a number of adult males. She was arrested for being drunk and disorderly (her conviction was later set aside) and none of the males were arrested. Child H was at this point identified as being at high risk of CSE. Risky Business, social care workers and the Police worked to support Child H and her father and she was looked after for a period. She suffered a miscarriage while with foster carers. Her family moved out of the area and Child H returned home. Some of the perpetrators were subsequently convicted.

5.31 **Child I (2009)** was 11 years old when she was raped and sexually assaulted. Her attacker was convicted. Her older sister was a victim of CSE. Child I regularly went missing and was subjected to rape and sexual assaults by older males. She became a looked after child because of concerns for her safety. She was further abused and exploited while she was looked after. She was placed out-of-area and repeatedly went missing, trying to get back to Rotherham. This made her even more vulnerable and she was repeatedly abused. She suffered post-traumatic stress disorder, self-harmed and at times became suicidal. Child I continues to be supported but despite the best efforts of children's social care services, the trauma she has suffered has resulted in lasting emotional and psychological damage.

5.32 **Child J (2009)** had a long history of neglect and child protection. She was 11 years old when she was identified as being at risk of sexual exploitation as well as sexual abuse within her family. Her older sister was a victim of sexual exploitation and the perpetrators were successfully prosecuted. Key information about Child J is missing from the electronic social care file. When she was 14 years old it was suspected she was visiting the homes of adult male strangers and possibly coercing other children to accompany her. A Strategy meeting chairperson clearly identified action that needed to be taken to protect Child J. There is no evidence on the file that appropriate action was taken. There was virtually nothing recorded on the file about the risks she faced, despite information being held elsewhere in children's social care that she was accompanying her older sister to high-risk situations where she was exposed to exploitation by adult males.

5.33 **Child K (2011)** was groomed by a known sex offender via Facebook when she was 13. Around that time, she required treatment at Accident and Emergency when she was taken there in an extremely intoxicated state. Since then, there has been a pattern of high-risk behaviour, with Child K having older boyfriends who are vulnerable. She frequents known hotspots with other young people at risk. She has been missing with other children although her parents do not report this and do not know where she is. Child K is very resistant to accepting help from the CSE team who tried hard to engage with her and her family and to offer support to prevent further sexual exploitation.

5.34 **Children L and M (2012)** were two young people from a minority ethnic community. They were part of a group of children who were at risk of sexual exploitation, investigated by the Police as part of Operation Carrington. A number of children at the same school were reported to be getting into cars with strangers, and getting paid in return for performing sex acts. Child L and Child M had frequent missing episodes and their families struggled to report them missing. This was partly because of language difficulties, but also because of cultural factors. The two children were at high risk of exploitation. The CSE team worked hard to engage with these young people and their families, to communicate the risks of sexual exploitation and provide them with education through group work and on a one to one basis. These two cases highlight the extreme difficulty of supporting children and their families when there are major language and cultural barriers, as a result of which neither the child nor parent is willing to disclose what is happening. The Police and social care workers in the CSE team were acutely aware of these difficulties and worked hard to overcome them.

5.35 **Child N (2013)** was 12 when extremely indecent images of her were discovered on the phones of fellow students. There were suspicions that older men and one woman had groomed her via Facebook. Her family were very shocked by photos and video images that had been taken of her, and have co-operated fully with the Police and the support offered by the CSE team. Child N was very angry at the agencies trying to help her. She showed no understanding of the risks of online contact with strangers and was not willing to disclose anything about those who have groomed and exploited her.

5.36 **Child O (2013)** was 13 when concerns about sexual exploitation emerged. She was wandering around Rotherham late at night, often in the company of an older girl who was a known victim of sexual exploitation. She was found in Sheffield on one occasion. She was often angry and violent towards family members, and they did not seem able to protect her. She was very active on social media sites and had acquired many adult associates whom she perceived to be her friends. She posted information online about a video she had seen of another child being sexually assaulted. The suspected perpetrator made contact with her and threatened if she said anything she would be the next victim. She was beaten up but neither she nor her parents were willing to disclose this to the Police. The risks to Child O were understood and documented by the CSE team, and a programme of preventive work was put in place. Nevertheless, Child O remained secretive about where she was when missing and whom she associated with. She continued to be at risk of exploitation.

Outcomes

5.37 It is important to emphasise that even when agencies intervened appropriately to protect and support children and young people, the impact sexual exploitation had on them was absolutely devastating. Time and again we read in the files and other documents of children being violently raped, beaten, forced to perform sex acts in taxis and cars when they were being trafficked between towns, and serially abused by large numbers of men. Many children repeatedly self-harmed and some became suicidal. They suffered family breakdown and some became homeless. Several years after they had been abused, a disproportionate number were victims of domestic violence, had developed long-standing drug and alcohol addiction, and had parenting difficulties with their own children, resulting in child protection/children in need interventions. Some suffered post-traumatic stress and other emotional and psychological problems, often undiagnosed and untreated. Some experienced mental health problems.

5.38 With a very small number of exceptions, there was little or no specialist counselling or appropriate mental health intervention offered to child victims, despite their acute distress. In those cases where psychological or psychiatric assessments were carried out, children were diagnosed as suffering severe post-traumatic stress. Specialist assessments also identified that where a child had on-going contact with a perpetrator, this was likely to be a direct result of the psychological damage that had been inflicted, rather than something the victim could control.

5.39 In a number of the cases we read, children and young people had pregnancies, miscarriages and terminations. Some had children removed under care orders and suffered further trauma when contact with their child was terminated and alternative family placements found. This affected not just the victims themselves, but other siblings who had developed attachments to the baby. However, there were other cases where vulnerable and sometimes very young mothers were able, with appropriate long-term support, to recover and successfully care for their children.

5.40 For the victims of sexual exploitation the judgment of outcomes therefore has to be qualified by recognition of what they have endured and the lasting harm this is likely to have caused to most of them.

5.41   For the reasons given above, there are very few good outcomes to be found in the files for the victims of sexual exploitation, even when the quality of intervention was good. This was true in some of the current open cases.

6. Children and Young People's Services

There was evidence of a good level of engagement with individual children, both by the Risky Business project and more recently by members of the CSE team. Children and their parents were consulted and kept informed. There was very good access to the services provided by Risky Business over many years through the outreach nature of their work. With the integration of the project into the CSE team, the capacity to provide open access was diminished. Several people expressed regret about this to the Inquiry.

Thresholds for social care had in the past been unacceptably high. While this had improved through the efforts of the co-located CSE team, there are currently insufficient resources in the team to meet all the demands made on it, and the team is unable to provide enough preventive input to sustain children after they have been exploited.

Risky Business made referrals to children's social care but in the early years, the response in terms of assessments, risk assessments and safeguarding was rarely good enough. At that time, there was a lack of clarity in inter-agency meetings that discussed individual children alongside more strategic issues, with no clear direction provided by senior managers.

In the historic cases, assessment and care planning by children's social care tended to be more systematic and of a higher standard for looked after children than for other children.

The quality of response by children's social care is better now than it was in the past in relation to assessment and care planning. However, there are weaknesses in risk assessment and risk management, which need to be addressed with some urgency.

Many of the current sexual exploitation cases are complex and time consuming, with the risk of staff resources becoming overstretched. Preventive work with children after incidents of exploitation is being squeezed. There has been a rise in online grooming and exploitation and this is placing new and challenging demands on services.

In the past, local residential units were targeted by perpetrators of sexual exploitation and were overwhelmed by the problem. Some children placed out-of-area for their own protection were failed by services. High priority should be given to adopting a more strategic approach to out of authority placements, and improving the quality of response to this group.

There are some excellent services in Rotherham including the Bridges project for care leavers, the Rowan Centre for school age mothers and a range of youth work services, although the latter had been reduced as a result of financial cutbacks.

Even today, there is little, if any, post-abuse counselling and support for victims. This is a major gap, given the long-term damage caused by sexual exploitation.

Engagement with Children and Young People[7]

6.1   There was evidence of agencies engaging positively with children and young people, both historically through the Risky Business project and currently through the CSE team.   In 81% of the cases we scrutinised, children were seen on their own at key stages of assessment, care planning and delivery and they (or their parents) were consulted and kept informed.   There was evidence of services actively seeking to take the child's view into account in 79% of cases.

6.2   Children's social care used a child friendly workbook entitled 'Relationships and Staying Safe' to help children and their workers to discuss some of the complex issues around relationships and child sexual exploitation.   This was originally developed by the Risky Business project, and completed workbooks were in some of the files we read.   This was an excellent and practical example of engagement with children to help them understand risks and keep themselves safe.

Access to Services

6.3   Access to Risky Business services over the years appeared in the main to have been good.   The project received referrals from the Police, children's social care, schools and health workers.   Parents and their children also self-referred to the project.   For example, over the 18 month period January 2004–June 2005, 35% of Risky Business referrals were from children's social care, 20% were self-referrals or referrals by parents, 9% were from the Police and 7% were from schools.   This fluctuated from year to year.   Sometimes the Police were the main source of referrals, and at other times, schools.

6.4   Historically, access to children's social care was much more problematic.   In part, this was because Risky Business was viewed as the main service for children who were being sexually exploited, with the result that children and young people were often signposted to Risky Business at the stage of initial contact, rather than being routed through Strategy meetings and S47[8] enquiries.

6.5   Inspection reports described how over many years, children's social care services were typically understaffed and overstretched, and struggling to cope with demand.

6.6   There was evidence in many files that prior to 2007, child victims from around the age of eleven upwards were not seen to be the priority for children's social care, even when they were being sexually abused and exploited.   The emphasis on protection of very young children to the exclusion of CSE victims has been identified in other reports[9] as a national trend rather than a Rotherham specific issue.

---

[7] Percentages given throughout this chapter are for all files read. Figures for current files are given in brackets where these are noticeably different.

[8] Section 47 of the Children Act 1989 places a duty on LAs to investigate and make inquiries into the circumstances of children considered to be at risk of 'significant harm' and, where these inquiries indicate the need, to decide what action, if any, it may need to take to safeguard and promote the child's welfare.

[9] E.g. Rochdale serious case reviews

Nevertheless, this lack of priority resulted in many Rotherham children failing to get the help and protection they needed.

6.7   The outreach nature of the Risky Business project meant that sexual exploitation was visible as a problem in Rotherham from the late 1990s. The CSE team has some capacity to provide outreach, and this is of a high standard. Members of the team confirmed that at the present time there is no pro-active service that is accessible and has the capacity to reach out to children who are being exploited but are not yet in contact with services.

6.8   We were told by the Executive Director of Strategic Services that the Integrated Youth Support Service provided outreach support to vulnerable young people who have been exploited or are at risk of CSE. However, youth workers told us that preventive work they had previously carried out with vulnerable groups of female and male teenagers, including those from minority ethnic communities, was no longer offered because of cutbacks. Work was in progress for IYSS to have a greater involvement with the CSE team in order to improve access to sexual health services.

6.9   The Inquiry concluded that an important dimension of the services offered in the past by Risky Business had been reduced or possibly lost. Accessibility is one of the key elements in reaching out to children who are sexually exploited or being groomed, and this needs to be done in ways that young people will engage with and trust. Every effort should be made to increase this capacity, building on the work currently done by youth workers and the GROW[10] worker in the CSE team. This is important because sexual exploitation by its very nature tends to be a hidden problem.

Assessment and Care Planning

6.10   Over the years, assessment and care planning attracted negative comment in many of the inspections of Rotherham children's social care.

6.11   The figures given in this chapter cover historic social care files, Risky Business files and cases currently open to children's social care. We comment on the current position where it differs significantly from the overall.

6.12   Many of the Risky Business files we read demonstrated a good level of care planning, with written goals and progress towards them recorded in a systematic way. The figures and ratings given in this chapter cover Risky Business and social care historic files, taken together. Without the Risky Business files, the ratings given below would have been poorer.

6.13   Historically and at the present time, assessment and care planning was systematic if

---

[10] GROW (Women Making Informed Choices) is a local voluntary organisation. Its INVOLVE project is focused on CSE. It employs a worker who is based in the joint CSE team. The GROW worker provides one-to-one emotional and practical support, helps to enable and support disclosures of CSE, and offers further support during investigations and prosecutions.

a child was looked after. In historic cases, the quality of assessment and care planning for looked after children was markedly better than for other children, where assessments were often weak, unsatisfactory or missing from the files. It was commonplace to find no care plan if children were not looked after or subject to child protection procedures. Chronologies were evident only as part of the preparation for court proceedings.

6.14 There was evidence of improved practice in assessment and care planning in the open cases in our sample.

6.15 There was a chronology in fewer than half the cases (43%) where it would have been appropriate to have one – and most chronologies were out of date, with significant gaps. It is likely that the absence of structured chronologies contributed to key information being missed when decisions were made.

6.16 There was an assessment on file in 73% of cases (n=44)[11]. The timing of the most recent assessment was in keeping with the needs of the child in over 71% (n=34) of cases. There was an assessment on file in all of the 23 currently open cases that we read.

6.17 The overall quality of assessments was good or very good in 63% of all cases, adequate in 23% and weak or unsatisfactory in 14%. The quality of assessments in open cases was good or very good in 76% of cases and adequate in the remaining 24%.

6.18 There was a care plan on file in 63% of cases (n=40), 80% for open cases. There was evidence that the services and care received by the young person followed the content of the care plan in over 90% of cases. Where there was a care plan, it mostly set out the desired outcomes for the child or young person (74% care plans), and there were SMART[12] objectives in 75% of care plans.

6.19 In some of the current and recently closed cases that we read, there seemed to be a presumption that short-term intervention was an appropriate response. For example some children were offered attendance at one or two group sessions designed to raise awareness of CSE. However, once there is evidence that a child has been sexually exploited, the presumption should be that the child and his/her family are likely to need sustained support and safeguarding over a considerable period of time, to make sure the child is protected.

6.20 We noted that in the final quarter of 2013, a third of the CSE team's cases had been closed. This was a high turnover of cases in a short period, and required further management investigation. We read seven of these cases, and judged that several of them had been closed prematurely, without all risks being adequately addressed.

---

[11] n= the number of cases where it was possible to give a rating
[12] SMART = objectives that are specific, measurable, achievable, realistic and time related.

In these instances the children could have benefited from longer term intervention by the CSE team.

6.21 We met children's social care staff and police officers in the joint CSE team. They were child-focused, enthusiastic and clearly committed to the safeguarding of exploited and at risk children. They described the pressures and stresses of dealing with child sexual exploitation. They told us that they did not feel under pressure to close individual cases. Nevertheless they acknowledged that the level of on-going preventive work they were able to offer children once the immediate risk of sexual exploitation had been addressed was far less than they would wish.

6.22 Managers need to give further attention to making sure there is an appropriate level of resources available to support continuing preventive work with children who have been exploited, especially in cases where the child or his/her parents would be unlikely to disclose behaviours that would put the child at risk of harm.

6.23 The volume of new work being handled by the CSE team was significant, and the team manager felt under pressure to ensure that there was throughput of work, so that new cases could be allocated. The team also co-worked cases with staff in other parts of children's social care, when their input was required, and they did a considerable amount of preventive work with schools and with a range of community groups.

6.24 Many of the individual cases were complex and time consuming, with the risk of staff resources becoming overstretched, and preventive work with children after incidents of exploitation was being squeezed. There was a rise in online grooming and exploitation that was placing new and challenging demands on services, and these cases too were complex and high risk.

6.25 Several managers commented to us that the present situation was not sustainable in terms of the wide range of expectations and pressures on the CSE team. This was not a view shared by the Executive Director of Children's Services. Nevertheless, this issue featured in the findings and recommendations of two recent independent reviews [13]. The Inquiry considers it imperative that issues around the remit, management and workload of the CSE team are properly addressed. For this reason we have included a further recommendation on this subject in this report.

Risk Assessment and Management

6.26 Historically, Risky Business used a standard reporting format to record judgements about risk. These were not available in all cases, but the risk forms we saw on the project's files were of an acceptable quality.

6.27 In the historic children's social care files, it was clear that the risks associated with

---

[13] Barnardo's Rotherham Practice Review (October 2013) and the Safeguarding Board's 'Review of the response to child sexual exploitation in Rotherham' (December 2013) – both described in Chapter 3

child sexual exploitation were in the main not well understood or responded to. This improved from around 2007, and a further marked improvement was evident from 2010. Prior to 2007, it was exceptional to find a risk assessment in the case files, and minutes of Strategy meetings suggested that children's social care and the Police adopted an approach of minimal intervention.

6.28   Prior to 2012, minutes of Strategy meetings about child sexual exploitation were held centrally and were not recorded on the child's social care file. This was a seriously flawed system and children's social care managers should be credited with changing it in 2012.

6.29   The Sexual Exploitation Forum started meeting around late 2003 and discussed individual children up until around 2007. Again, there was no record of these discussions and decisions on the child's file. Front line workers and managers responsible for the case would not have been present at such meetings. This led to confusion between the strategic responses to sexual exploitation and risk assessment and management in individual cases.

6.30   There was a risk assessment on file in 73% of cases. As with assessments and care plans, Risky Business and the current open cases pulled up the overall results. Overall, we judged the quality of risk assessments to be good or very good in 34% of cases, adequate in 17% of cases and weak or unsatisfactory in 47% of cases

6.31   When we examined current cases, there was a risk assessment on file in 59% of our sample. The proportion of missing assessments (41%) was unacceptably high. The proportion judged to be good quality was 18%, 27% were judged to be adequate and 54% were weak or unsatisfactory.

6.32   When we looked at the extent to which risk had been identified, responded to and reduced in currently open cases, the results were more encouraging. 75% were judged to be adequate or better. This suggests to us that there was a better standard of professional judgements and response to risk than was apparent from the quality of the risk assessments on the files.

6.33   Work was already in progress to improve the quality and consistency of risk assessments. An operational protocol had been agreed by Children and Young People's Services and the Police and was approved by the CSE sub-group in June 2014. This built on learning from audits of CSE cases (described in Chapter 7) and set clear responsibilities and timescales for risk assessments to be completed in open and new cases. It formalised the arrangement that risk assessments would always be carried out jointly by children's social care and the Police, as is current practice in the joint CSE team. The protocol also introduced regular sampling of risk assessments by managers.

6.34   We raised concerns with senior managers about two open and two historic cases where we considered the quality of risk management and decision making to have been extremely poor. In one of the historic cases, a disclosure made by the child five years ago was in the file but appeared not to have been actioned or reported to the Police. This required further investigation by the Council and we understand this is already taking place.

6.35 We also reviewed two historic and three open cases with a specialist team from the National Working Group Network. In the three open cases, there was a clear consensus between the Inquiry file reader and the National Working Group Network that the risk was considerably higher than that suggested by the numeric scoring tool and recorded on file.

6.36 We read several open cases where children were looked after out-of-area, one of which was reviewed in detail with a team from the National Working Group Network. We recommended to senior managers that there should be an externally facilitated review of one of these cases so that there could be learning by all agencies from this case.

6.37 We concluded that there were significant weaknesses in risk assessment and risk management. These should be addressed if children are to be properly safeguarded. In particular, high priority should be given to making sure that there is a risk assessment on the file of every child at risk of sexual exploitation. Management action was needed to improve the quality of risk assessments. This should build on some very good audit work that has already been undertaken.

Risk Assessment Tool

6.38 Joint assessments were carried out by social workers and police officers in the joint CSE team. The risk assessment tool is based on a widely used numeric scoring system. It was based on the Barnardo's best practice model and adopted across South Yorkshire in October 2013.

6.39 Staff in the CSE team were child-focused, enthusiastic and clearly committed to the safeguarding of exploited and at risk children. They reported difficulty in reconciling the outcome of the numeric scoring system with their professional judgements of risk and singled out the sexual health section as being particularly problematic.

6.40 The manager of the CSE team and social workers in the team said that they struggled to use the risk assessment tool, because it recorded risks only where there was hard evidence. This meant that sometimes children they considered to be at risk had scores that were too low.

6.41 The numeric scoring tool should be kept under very close review. A particular area of concern is that workers and the CSE team manager reported to us that they find it difficult to capture risks using the numeric tool. We read a significant number of cases in which the numeric risk assessment tool understated the risks to the child.

6.42 Gathering information in CSE cases is difficult for a number of reasons, including the possibility that children may not see themselves as victims and may be reluctant to disclose, or there is denial on the part of parents. Lack of hard evidence should not equate to an assumption of no risk or low risk, especially if a child has a history of being exploited and is unable to disclose what he/she is experiencing.

6.43 We discussed the risk assessment tool with representatives of the Police and children's social care, as well as with operational managers and staff working in the CSE team. Managers were clear that the numeric scoring system was an aid to, but did not replace, professional judgements about risk. This is clearly stated in the recently approved operational procedure. We were told that work had been undertaken on the risk assessment tool to address the tensions between numeric scoring and professional judgement. This involved amending some categories and allowing for the assessor to override the score where necessary.

6.44 Operational managers were confident that management decisions and professional judgements would be used to adjust the level of risk where necessary. We were told that risk was not measured solely by the numeric scoring tool. At the time of the Inquiry, there was not as yet a system for making sure that this was clearly recorded in the risk assessment stored on the child's electronic case file. It is essential that the child's file clearly records the most up-to-date professional judgement of risk, especially when this may be higher than the score recorded on the numeric tool. We were told that changes have now been made to introduce a dialogue box and that risk assessments are collated by the police analyst using a software analytical tool.

6.45 Some very good work was in progress to improve the management of high-risk cases. The joint CSE team had established a Group Assessment and Progression (GAP). This group met regularly to oversee and review risk assessment and risk management of all high-risk cases. The police analyst was supporting the work of this group. We examined the minutes of one GAP meeting, and considered that there had been very thorough discussions about the children's needs and the risks they faced.

6.46 The recently approved operational protocol ensured that social workers responsible for the child were invited to attend the GAP meeting. It is imperative that in all cases a note of this GAP discussion is entered in the risk assessment section of the child's case file. The responsibility for this needs to be clearly defined, so that the most recent information about risk is always available to those accessing the child's file.

6.47 We refer to quality assurance and continuous improvement in the next chapter and how some excellent audit work is helping to improve performance on risk. The implementation of the new operational procedures will require close monitoring. Sampling of CSE cases should be carried out until such time as there is evidence of improved consistency and quality in the assessment and management of risk.

Services for Looked After Children

6.48   From the mid-1990s there were concerns about children's homes being targeted for the purposes of child sexual exploitation. From the residential case files we read, it is clear that for a long period thereafter some local residential units were overwhelmed by the problem of child sexual exploitation. Children who were exploited before they became looked after continued to be exploited, and were often at even greater risk of harm. Other children became exposed to sexual exploitation for the first time whilst they were looked after in children's homes. There were examples of an exploited child acting as the conduit for perpetrators to gain access to other looked after children. This happened in local residential units as well as in out-of-area placements, and it appears to have occurred in one of the current cases we read. There was no appropriate management response to the problem of children being exposed to exploitation whilst in the care of the Council. Nor did we find that elected members as corporate parents were advised of the scale and gravity of the problem.

6.49   Historically, information about looked after children affected by CSE is patchy. There was not yet a well-developed system for tracking the impact of CSE on them. One reason for this may be that operational managers believed that CSE should be managed through 'looked after children processes'. For example, in July 2005, 90 children were being discussed by the Sexual Exploitation Forum. A management decision was taken to remove from the list all children who were looked after or on the child protection register. A standard letter was to be sent to their social workers reminding them to consider sexual exploitation in future work with the child. With hindsight, this was a serious error of judgement. Services for looked after children were stretched at the time and practice was uneven. It was unlikely that frontline staff had the knowledge or skills to deal with organised sexual exploitation. It also made it impossible to gauge the nature and scale of the problem, particularly in residential units.

6.50   One response, then and now, was to place children in residential units outside the Rotherham area, in the hope that this would reduce the risk of harm from sexual exploitation. We read some cases where this had been successful for particular children. There were examples of children being placed in secure care as the last and only option to protect them from perpetrators, and in several cases such a placement proved to be beneficial in protecting the children and in creating the opportunity to work therapeutically with them. There were also examples of out-of-area foster placements being very positive for the children. However, there were many examples of out-of-area residential placements actually increasing the risks to exploited children, with an escalation of missing episodes as they tried to return to their home and sometimes to their abusers.

6.51   In July 2014, there were 16 children who were looked after on account of sexual exploitation. Six were in out-of-area placements (one in secure care and another waiting for a secure placement). Three were in out-of-area foster placements; and three in 'in-house' (local) foster placements. One of the 16 children was at home; another in an in-house residential placement; and two in semi-independent living arrangements.

6.52 A strategic approach to protecting looked after children who are sexually exploited, or at risk, should now be addressed as a matter of urgency by the Child Sexual Exploitation sub-group. The strategy should aim to ensure that out-of-area placements do much more than simply move the problem elsewhere. It should identify the current range of services available for children who are exploited or at serious risk; and identify the contribution of foster-carers, substitute families, secure care and local residential units. It should include risk-assessing potential placements for the individual child and for other vulnerable children. The strategy should also be bound into the Council's role as corporate parents.

6.53 This is not an issue that Rotherham can deal with on its own. Cross-boundary solutions must be found. Children who are exploited are routinely being placed in out-of-area placements across the country. Unless Councils can develop sound strategic agreements with other authorities, these children will continue to be exploited and abused, and may become the conduit for perpetrators to gain access to other children in the same placement.

Leaving Care Services

6.54 Services provided by the Bridges project[14] were of a high quality over many years, and workers had a great deal of experience of supporting children who had been sexually exploited. After-care workers told us that from their perspective, the quality of support for exploited children had improved greatly in recently years. The project received very good support from the managers of the CSE team, both children's social care and the Police. After-care workers also commented that children who had been looked after out of the authority faced major difficulties at the point of leaving care. They found it difficult to get support in the area where they had been living, and had great difficulty re-settling in Rotherham, which was often their only option if they required assistance with housing and other supports. Again, this should form part of a strategic approach to meeting the needs of looked after children who are affected by child sexual exploitation.

Youth Services

6.55 Historically, Rotherham had a good network of local youth services that was part of the range of preventive services accessed by children who were exploited or at risk. Youth Services played an important role in identifying and supporting children and young people involved in or at risk of CSE. The wider youth service was also active in this area, with projects such as the Youth Start counselling service. This was a valuable resource for many children affected by sexual exploitation.

---

[14] The Bridges project was provided by NCH until April 2014, when it transferred to the Council.

6.56   The Cabinet considered a review of Youth Services in February 2011. Under 'Risks and Uncertainties', the report stated:

> 'Without this integrated working, we risk retreating again into silos of provision to tackle some of our most stubborn challenges - youth crime, teenage pregnancies, NEETs [15] , sexual exploitation, adolescent drinking and associated disorder. Past experience and current evidence tell us that this is much less effective, and in many cases pointless'.

6.57   We met several experienced and skilled youth workers who voiced serious concerns about the severity of the cutbacks in the youth services and specifically how it was impacting on their work with vulnerable young people.

Services for Young Mothers

6.58   The Rowan Centre provides education, support and childcare to pregnant schoolgirls and young mothers from the Rotherham area. Babies are cared for on-site during the day whilst mothers receive their education.

6.59   We read the case files of several CSE victims who received education and support from the Rowan Centre. It was clear that the Centre provided a highly personalised, child-focused approach and was able to engage with, and support, girls who had become pregnant while they were being sexually exploited. The Centre had been a positive experience for these girls, several of whom were able with support to successfully parent their children. There was also evidence of good collaboration between the Risky Business project and the Centre, with both services providing support to victims for as long as this was required.

6.60   There were historic and current issues regarding liaison between the Rowan Centre and children's social care. It was evident from several historic files that there was tension around the thresholds that children's social care applied. As a result children who were considered highly vulnerable by the Centre did not get help. Staff at the Centre told us that high thresholds for social care mean that some pregnant girls and young mothers do not currently receive the support they need.

6.61   To address these issues, children's social care should introduce a mechanism for reviewing cases with the Rowan Centre where there is a difference of opinion about priority.

Post Abuse Support

6.62   There appeared to be very little by way of specialist support services, in the form of mental health, counselling and psychological services for children and young people

---

[15] Not in Education, Employment or Training

who had been sexually exploited. Many suffered post-traumatic stress and endured lasting psychological and emotional damage that diminished their capacity to lead normal lives. One survivor told us:

"Sexual exploitation is like a circle that you can never escape from."

6.63   We came across a number of cases where children and young people needed and wanted specialist counselling and support. They were unable to access services because of long waiting lists and gaps in services. We learned that at the time of the Inquiry, the Children and Adolescent Mental Health Service (CAMHS) deleted children's names from the waiting list if they missed the first appointment. This approach is entirely unsuited to the needs of CSE victims and it should be changed. We were told by the parent of a survivor who needed help when she was over 16 that he had to pay privately for this service, as there was at least a six month waiting list for an appointment. This was too long in the life of a young woman who had experienced such trauma.

7. Safeguarding

Over the years, there were good inter-agency structures in place to deal with sexual exploitation. As early as 1998, police procedures, also adopted by children's social care, identified the victims as children and the prosecution of perpetrators as a priority. Under the auspices of the Safeguarding Board and its predecessor, the Area Child Protection Committee, there was a good range of strategies, policies and procedures applicable to child protection and specifically to CSE. These were of generally good quality and had been developed on an inter-agency basis. The weakness was that the Safeguarding Board rarely seemed to check whether they were being implemented and whether they were working. The challenge function of the Safeguarding Board did not appear to have been fully exercised.

Over many years an impressive amount of training on CSE was carried out, encompassing a wide spectrum of interests in the community.

From 2008 onwards, annual CSE plans were produced and presented to the Safeguarding Board and to the Lead Member for Children and Young People.

The Child S Serious Case Review commissioned by the Safeguarding Board sparked a debate about redactions in such reports and whether absolute transparency should take precedence over protecting the confidential details of children. Whilst we agreed that some of the redactions in the Child S review were unnecessary or could have been differently presented, we did not believe that a charge of 'cover up' by the Safeguarding Board was justified.

Strategies, Policies and Procedures

7.1   The Children Act 2004 established Local Safeguarding Children Boards. They bring organisations together to safeguard and promote the welfare of children through mutual co-operation. They are required to co-ordinate and ensure the effectiveness of their members' services, to develop policies and procedures for the safeguarding of children, to undertake reviews of serious cases and to produce an annual report. The range of their responsibilities extends to training, recruitment, publicity and the setting of thresholds for intervention. While Safeguarding Boards do not have the power to direct other organisations, they do have a role in making clear where improvement is needed.

7.2   Prior to the establishment of Safeguarding Boards in 2004, the principal responsibilities were undertaken by Area Child Protection Committees (ACPCs). The Inquiry had access to minutes of the Safeguarding Board, We saw very few of the Area Child Protection Committee minutes. Approximately 40 sets of minutes from both were read.

7.3   There were good inter-agency structures to deal with CSE over the period covered by the Inquiry. These linked in to the Safeguarding Board or its predecessor. Officer groups included the Key Players (late '90s to around 2003), the Sexual Exploitation Forum, the Sexual Exploitation Steering Group and the current Safeguarding Board CSE sub-group, which is supported by an operational 'Silver' group.

7.4   We also read minutes of the Sexual Exploitation Forum and the current CSE sub-group. Neither the Council nor the Police were able to trace minutes of the Key Players meeting. This is particularly troubling because the minutes included records of decision making in individual cases. These minutes, or relevant extracts from them, were not placed in individual children's social care files. This means that children who want information about their past, in terms of what happened to them and why, would be denied this information.

7.5   One of the major flaws in inter-agency meetings in the early years was confusion of responsibilities for strategic responses and decision making on individual children. This persisted until around 2007, when a dedicated manager for CSE was appointed.

7.6   The Safeguarding Board and the Area Child Protection Committee did a considerable amount of work in developing inter-agency strategies, policies and protocols on safeguarding and CSE from as early as 2001. They also oversaw the provision of extensive training.

7.7   Strategies, polices and procedures were developed within the framework of Government guidance in 'Working Together to Safeguard Children' and extensive work was done on issues such as:

a) children's safety – an inter-agency steering group was established in 2005 following a report on bullying and racism in schools and took forward a number of initiatives to improve children's safety; and

b) domestic violence – a strategy was developed in 2006 and took forward work on 'Hidden Harm' (protecting children from drug misusing parents and carers)

7.8   As early as 1998, South Yorkshire Police issued a paper 'Protecting children who are being sexually exploited through prostitution'. Its procedures governed the practice of the Police and were adopted by children's social care. The paper clearly set out the risks to the physical, emotional and psychological health of children who engaged in prostitution or were victims of sexual exploitation. It recognised the links between prostitution and crime, drug abuse, violence and murder, and urged that a high priority be given to the problem. Children under the age of 18 were to be regarded as 'children in need', protected under law. The priority for the Police was to identify and prosecute offenders. There is evidence from this Inquiry that suggests that these precepts were not always followed.

7.9   By April 2001, the Area Child Protection Committee procedures included a chapter 'Protecting children who are being sexually abused through prostitution'. The procedures largely reiterated those of 1998. They were revised in 2003.

7.10   A report to the Safeguarding Board in 2005 repeated the statement in the child abuse procedures that 'prostitution is a form of sexual exploitation involving payment or reward'. The implied equivalence of child sexual exploitation with child prostitution was common in the 1990s and should not have persisted until 2005. It suggested that payment or reward was always involved and it made no mention of the criminal nature of the activity. It might even imply that the child's consent mitigated its gravity.

7.11 The Safeguarding Board frequently sought an agreed, practical definition of child sexual exploitation in order to ensure consistency of approach by its members. Even as late as October 2013, the CSE sub-group was discussing concerns about the distinction between sexual abuse and sexual exploitation, fearing that the terms were used interchangeably. At the very least, disparities would affect the accuracy of performance figures, but they might have had more profound implications for practice.

Missing Children

7.12 The protocol on Missing Children, launched in 2005, aimed to focus agencies' minds on the risks to which such children were exposed. They undertook responsibility for managing its implementation and reviewing it in the light of experience. The protocol was 'decentralised' into local strategies with a view to engaging General Practitioners, Accident and Emergency Departments and community groups. Local campaigns were envisaged, overseen by those working in each area. Rotherham was the only policing district in the Force to respond formally to the problem, through its Community Safety Unit, by visiting young 'runaways' when they returned.

7.13 The Action Plan on Missing Children was frequently reviewed in subsequent years. The Police submitted regular statistical evidence. In 2008, the Children and Young People's Scrutiny Panel discussed the topic. The following year, Rotherham scored 14 out of a possible 15, based on a self-assessment against national indicators.

7.14 Agencies worked together on possible links between missing children and sexual exploitation. An official visited schools to talk to year-6 pupils about running away. An inter-agency Action Group met frequently to maintain a watching brief. The Borough commissioned the charity Safe@Last to interview children who had been missing. Many missing children were identified through fraudulent benefit claims. The subject featured large in the work plan, which the Exploitation sub-group submitted in 2010. The plan engaged voluntary and other agencies in addressing the problem that had become more severe in Rotherham over recent years. The Borough's proportion of missing looked-after children was higher than the national average, and there had been a sharp increase in the numbers of missing children in their mid-teens.

Plans to Tackle Sexual Exploitation

7.15 At the end of 2005, the Safeguarding Board approved a comprehensive action plan which covered inter-agency planning and procedures; work in schools; preventive methodologies; the provision of advice to young people; services to young men and boys at risk of sexual exploitation; systems of recording and analysis; the gathering of evidence and the support of child witnesses. Sexual exploitation was regarded as a priority in the Stay Safe section of the Children and Young People's single plan.

7.16 'Responding to Sexual Exploitation in Rotherham', compiled by the Police and children's social care in 2005, imposed the common assessment form on referrals, set up Strategy meetings on cases of significant harm, and stressed the importance of identifying all adults involved in any referral. The paper retained the clause giving advice to the young person on two occasions before proceeding to caution or prosecution; also the clause making a case conference dependent on the parent's having encouraged the young person's behaviour. It reiterated the need to 'investigate and prosecute those who coerce, exploit or abuse children'.

7.17 In October 2006, the multi-agency sexual exploitation procedures had been completed and circulated. Almost all of the specific objectives of the comprehensive action plan had been achieved. Membership of the group overseeing the action plan had been enlarged to include the voluntary sector and health services.

7.18 In 2008, the Safeguarding Board began to formulate policies and procedures relating to the exploitation of boys and young men. Concern about this issue had been expressed as far back as 2002. A staff member was now deployed to research the nature, context and extent of the exploitation, the degree to which boys were affected, and the range of services that should be provided.

7.19 Over the following months, procedures were compiled or revised on missing children, children who were trafficked, children who harm others, and safeguarding girls and young women at risk of abuse through genital mutilation. 'Safeguarding Children Guidance' was a new policy designed for Madrassahs, Mosques and supplementary schools. In 2009, it was proposed that the procedures relating to CSE should be revised to conform to new national guidance on the safeguarding of children. Sheffield had taken an initiative in this direction with a view to agreeing procedures common to both authorities. Later that year, Rotherham was described as having 'taken the most proactive approach to dealing with the issue of child sexual exploitation', compared with other areas. This assessment was endorsed by the findings of the Offender Management Inspection a couple of years later.

7.20 The Children and Young Person's Plan 2010-2013 brought together a number of inter-connected strategies under four broad headings: prevention, early intervention, tackling inequality and education. Strategies on organised or multiple abuse and sexual exploitation were tabled at this time.

7.21 In 2010, the Safeguarding Board approved further policies on the forced marriage of young people; honour-based violence; organised, multiple abuse; the management of people who pose a risk to young people; and safeguarding children from sexual exploitation. It was planned to update all policies and procedures twice a year. A company called TriX was commissioned to maintain the Safeguarding Board's library of policies and procedures.

7.22 Policies and procedures were revised again in 2011. It was intended that staff would refer to the procedures on-line rather than using paper versions. The website gave a single version of the procedures, regularly updated and accessible to all. In the same year, the Practice Resolution Protocol was developed in response to the need for a systematic process for challenging professional practice.

7.23 In December 2012, there were calls for a shared clear definition of referral processes and threshold criteria to be agreed by all agencies. This suggests that debates on these topics in 2005 and subsequent years remained unresolved. It was also proposed that a 'suitable shared multi-agency recording system' for CSE be devised, to include information about adults who may be linked to children at risk of abuse or exploitation.

Representation and Accountability

7.24 The current CSE sub-group has served to reduce a problem which has beset the Safeguarding Board from its early days - that of sheer size. In the interests of inclusiveness, Board membership has progressively increased. Fewer than 20 people attended its first meetings. As meetings become larger the more difficult it is for the Chair to give due weight to the varying interests represented, to encourage full and open debate and reach definitive conclusions which attract the agreement of all present. In addition, the Chair has the responsibility to ensure that decisions are acted upon, timeously and to a high standard. Not only does this make the task difficult for a part-time Chair, but it also raises questions about the concept of accountability as applied to such a large, disparate group of people. It is not the place of the Inquiry to explore those questions further. It is sufficient to be reminded that accountability for successful outcomes is a central feature of good child protection work. The concept of 'shared accountability' which some apply to the work of Safeguarding Boards is dubious and potentially dangerous.

7.25 The issue of thresholds typifies a problem which the Safeguarding Board and its predecessor faced from the early years - that of ensuring compliance with agreements on the part of all of its members. The child protection procedures and protocols produced during the late 1990s and early 2000s were of generally good quality, but adherence to them within the membership was variable. Similar problems attended the training programmes. Inter-agency training on CSE was instituted in the early 2000s, particularly on awareness raising. This was commended by the Leader of the Council who called for its extension, but the level of take-up was often low. Poor take-up was not universal, but its frequency called into question the authority that the Safeguarding Board exercised over its members. Likewise considerable time and energy was expended on devising good policies and procedures in the mid to late 2000s, but there was rarely any reporting back or checking by the Safeguarding Board on whether they were being implemented or were working.

Training

7.26   Under the Children Act 2004 and subsequent regulations, Local Safeguarding Children Boards have a responsibility towards the training of persons who work with children or in services affecting the safety and welfare of children. All agencies providing such services have a like responsibility to ensure their effectiveness through the provision of training. It is clear that the Safeguarding Board in Rotherham took this responsibility very seriously.

7.27   From the late 1990s onwards, Risky Business delivered training programmes on CSE for youth workers and others on an inter-agency basis. The training was coordinated through the Key Players group. Priority was given to a multi-agency model that would promote networking and help agencies to understand others' roles and responsibilities. The training sessions were well received, in particular training delivered by young survivors - this was described as having had a huge impact. The training was open to voluntary agencies and was well publicised.

7.28   Over the years, the Safeguarding Board faced a number of recurrent problems related to training. Agencies gave varying priority to the training; attendance was sometimes poor; the costs of the programme often exceeded its budget; it was difficult to recruit an adequate pool of trainers. In 2005, it was proposed that a charging system be introduced whereby agencies were billed for non-attendance.

7.29   The demand for training in CSE was ever increasing, as was its scope. The Leader's Task and Finish Group called for more awareness training, especially in CSE; the Safeguarding Board's training sub-committee undertook training around the conduct of serious case reviews; training in child protection was launched for mosque and community representatives; and housing, licensing and other staff were included in the programme. Risky Business even trained dog walkers and park rangers.

7.30   By the end of 2006 it was clear that the overall training programme could not be expanded unless capacity was increased, and the new budget meant the cancellation of 106 'trainer days' that had been delivered the previous year. In response, the Safeguarding Board made further efforts to impose a more structured method of identifying and meeting the needs for training within its membership.

7.31 The development of e-learning was encouraged. Members of the Safeguarding Board had all registered and viewed the course. The feedback was excellent. E-learning was considered to be valuable in meeting the needs for induction within isolated agencies that had limited access to training; it would also help residential staff who worked shifts. All agencies were asked to nominate staff who would benefit from e-learning, as part of their induction or refresher training.

7.32 In 2007, the Police asked Risky Business to contribute to the training of all newly recruited police officers. 3-day training courses were also delivered for senior police officers. The sexual exploitation of children featured in these programmes.

7.33 By 2008, the scope of the training programme had further increased to include safeguarding children with disabilities; the care of children with sexually harmful behaviour; the assessment of parental mental health; attachment theory; forced marriages and public law. Between 2007 and 2008, Risky Business delivered training on CSE to five comprehensive schools, to Police Community Safety Officers, to youth workers, to foster carers and to magistrates. In future, this training would form part of the standard package for all new magistrates. Many courses were now modular in form and more flexible than in the past. A training package was designed specifically for school staff to deliver, so spreading the material more widely and more economically.

7.34 By 2012, it seemed that child sexual exploitation had become a standard feature in the planning of training programmes. A training package in CSE was designed for Muslim community leaders; and the Safeguarding Board provided a training course in the identification of indicators relating to CSE. In March 2013, it was reported that all schools, including faith schools, had signed up for training related to CSE. Members of the Safeguarding Board devoted time to the discussion of the National Working Group Network's e-learning package on CSE.

Scrutiny and Challenge

7.35 Not unreasonably, the minutes of the Safeguarding Board meetings focus on decisions rather than the details of debate. Nevertheless, over the years there appears to have been a failure to challenge policies, priorities and performance, especially those of statutory agencies. This judgement featured in the Ofsted report of 2012 and was cited by the Home Affairs Select Committee. One task of the Board is to 'ensure effectiveness', to question, to scrutinise, to demand and assess evidence. In the past this function does not seem to have been fully exercised. The establishment of the CSE sub-group has gone some way to correcting this. Quality assurance has been strengthened, processes of performance monitoring and recording have improved, and clearer leadership demonstrated. In 2013, the incoming Board Chair commissioned his own 'diagnostic' of how CSE was being addressed, further confirming the intention to make the Board a more dynamic and mutually accountable body.

7.36   The parent of a CSE survivor was approached by a senior officer of the Council to become a lay member of the Safeguarding Board in 2010. He told the Inquiry that he found action on some important issues too slow, suggesting that the Board did not take the issue of CSE seriously enough. He reported that they had many good debates, but disagreement was never reflected in the minutes. He resigned from the Board in 2012.

7.37   While this report carries criticisms of the work of the Safeguarding Board over the last 10 years, the Inquiry considers that the several Chairs and members should be recognised for the work they have done, in the face of increased demand, frequent resourcing issues, and exposure to the attentions of the press and other media.

Compliance with Best Known Practice

7.38   We have seen that over the period covered in the Inquiry, there has been a fundamental shift at national as well as local level in the way child sexual exploitation is defined and understood. What was viewed in the late 1990s as the problem of child prostitution is now correctly defined as an issue of inter-agency responsibility for safeguarding children.

7.39   The Inquiry was asked to comment not just on best practice as understood today, but to reflect on whether past practice would have met the test of best known practice at that time.

7.40   There is little doubt that the Risky Business project and the Home Office research project that was underway in 2001/02 had a central focus on the safeguarding of children who were victims or at risk of sexual exploitation. The Risky Business project was ahead of its time. Some people we spoke to would argue that such a service could only be fully effective if it was located in the voluntary rather than the local authority sector.

7.41   Prior to 2007 the operational response of children's social care, together with that of the Police, would have fallen short of any accepted definition of best practice as understood at the time. One exception was the work of the Key Players group. Government guidance was clear at that time that CSE was to be dealt with as an issue of safeguarding children. However, many child victims in Rotherham were not dealt with through safeguarding procedures. From other reports[16] on the problem of

---

[16]http://www.nspcc.org.uk/Inform/resourcesforprofessionals/sexualabuse/sexual_exploitation_research_wda8513 0.html

child sexual exploitation, it would appear that this failure was not unique to Rotherham.

7.42   From about 2007, with the appointment of a dedicated manager for CSE, there was an improved focus on safeguarding children who were being exploited. This was evidenced in child sexual exploitation strategies and action plans and in a clear pathway for referral to children's social care. Nevertheless, safeguarding of individual children who were being exploited or at risk remained extremely variable. This was in line with wider weaknesses in the delivery of children's social care in Rotherham, evidenced in inspections over the years.

Supervision

7.43   Professional supervision of children's social care staff plays an important role in ensuring a high quality of social work practice and good case management. A comprehensive supervision policy should provide the employer and employee with a framework within which each will understand their obligations regarding accountability for work, professional development and personal support.

7.44   There is little information about the quality of supervision available to children's social care staff in the early years of the Inquiry period.

7.45   In 2008, Children and Young People's Services produced a report on casework supervision, outlining its role and function and why it was important. There was also a report to the Safeguarding Board in that year informing members that there had been an increase in the ratio of service managers to practitioners in order to improve quality through supervision and support.

7.46   By 2010, an Action Plan was in place to address the provision, frequency and quality of staff supervision.

7.47   In 2011, the Child S Serious Case Review made recommendations about the supervision of children's social care staff and youth services staff. The former required that all staff knew who was responsible for their case supervision and that there was clear accountability for their work. The latter referred to Risky Business staff, who should be the subject of greater management oversight and supervision. The Risky Business staff were incorporated in the central CSE team, following the publication of the Child S report.

7.48   Inspection reports on children's social care over the Inquiry period included several references to the quality and frequency of supervision. It was criticised in 2003 and 2009 and again in 2011, when Ofsted described it as 'variable' and sometimes 'poor'.

7.49   The workforce strategy developed by children's social care from 2010 seemed to be the first effective initiative taken to address the quality of supervision, particularly for newly qualified workers. The current supervision policy for social workers is clear, comprehensive and specific about frequency and content.

7.50 The evidence from file reading shows that in answer to the question 'Was the impact of worker supervision evident in the case file?', the impact of supervision was seen in 54% of all the cases we read, and in 88% of open cases. This demonstrates a good improvement over time in the quality of supervision provided to social work staff. However, it also shows the considerable shortfalls that existed in historic cases, where in some instances social workers must have lacked the necessary support to work effectively with very complex cases of sexual exploitation.

Quality Assurance and Continuous Improvement

7.51 Many of the cases we read were about a very serious level of sexual exploitation. It was striking that apart from a 'Lessons Learned' review, there appeared to have been no systems in place for agencies to learn lessons from serious CSE cases in which children had been failed. The apparent absence of active learning by any of the agencies in the most serious cases may have contributed to repetition of poor practice.

7.52 The 'Lessons Learned' review was produced during the Operation Central criminal trial. It was therefore not a full 'lessons learned' review. The intention was to follow it up after the criminal proceedings had finished. This does not appear to have happened. We also considered that the original review was weak in that it examined one case only, although charges were brought in respect of four children. There was also a much wider group of children identified in Operation Central who had been sexually exploited but whose cases did not get to court. It would have been appropriate to identify lessons to be learned from what happened with this group as well.

7.53 One of the potential areas for improvement should have been retrospective learning from the police operations Czar and Chard that failed to result in any prosecutions. We could find no evidence of agencies jointly reviewing what had happened in these cases, and learning lessons for the future.

7.54 At the time of the Inquiry, there was one post dedicated to quality assurance of safeguarding. Half this member of staff's time was spent working for the Safeguarding Board and the other half for children's social care. A case file audit tool had been developed. It was based on best practice elsewhere. The audit form had been revised and streamlined. It was comprehensive and well designed.

7.55 Different approaches to case file audits had been tested to find out what worked best. Children's social care carried out an audit of 14 child sexual exploitation cases in May 2014.

7.56   We examined two cases that had been recently audited and considered the audit process to be relevant, comprehensive and an example of good practice.

7.57   Learning is already underway as a result of the themed audit of CSE cases, particularly around the areas of:

   a) risk assessments missing in some cases;

   b) delay in updating risk assessments;

   c) quality of risk assessments; and

   d) examples of good practice.

7.58   The emphasis that Rotherham is now giving to quality assurance and continuous improvement in relation to child sexual exploitation is an extremely positive development. The achievements to date are considerable and we recommend that those in authority ensure that quality assurance work in respect of CSE will continue to be appropriately resourced and supported, as a key factor in practice improvement.

Serious Case Review

7.59   The Safeguarding Board commissioned only one Serious Case review involving CSE. That was the report on Child S, who was murdered in 2010 at the age of 17. There has been some dispute over the motivation for her murder, and whether CSE played any part in it. There is no doubt she was at risk of CSE when she was young and that she had been in contact with some of the worst perpetrators.

7.60   The author, Professor Pat Cantrill, was asked by the Safeguarding Board to examine the victim's circumstances and the services' response from 2008. The Safeguarding Board requested that the report be redacted to protect the children involved, prior to publication, and Professor Cantrill carried out the redactions herself.

7.61   The question of redactions in this report became very contentious and directly involved the former Secretary of State for Education, Michael Gove. He wrote to the Safeguarding Board to say that some of the redactions were unnecessary. There followed an unedifying set of exchanges between the Department for Education (DfE) and the Chair of the Safeguarding Board. At one point, the DfE lost a copy of the Serious Case Review.   This contained revised redactions completed by the Safeguarding Board.

7.62   Any review of services provided to protect children from physical and sexual abuse and exploitation is undoubtedly and properly a matter of public interest. However, the public interest must be balanced against considerations of the future well-being of any children and young people mentioned in the review. The Overview report on Child S had two principal purposes; first to describe and assess the conduct of the professionals and others who had a responsibility towards her and her family, and second to indicate clearly the lessons to be learned so that such tragic events would be prevented in future. For both purposes, the paramount concern must be for the welfare of children.

7.63   The young people in the family concerned had their lives ahead of them. We should help them to put aspects of their past behind them and develop into responsible citizens. The Overview report talked of many aspects of their lives in some detail. It is our strong view that it would not be beneficial that this should be put into the public domain and remain there for evermore. For most of the children's 'misdemeanours' no formal charges were laid. The unredacted report therefore discloses information that would otherwise be protected.

7.64   This is a difficult issue, which merits serious debate. The Home Affairs Select Committee has recommended that 'the victim, or their family, or an independent person' should have the right of redaction of serious case reviews. We recommend that the Department of Education should not demand the removal of redactions without giving thought to the implications for all of the children concerned. Whatever policy is determined on redactions, nothing must be allowed to inhibit the author of the report or detract from the honesty and integrity of the review and its findings.

7.65   The selection of redactions is a matter of judgement. In alleging a 'cover-up', the Times newspaper cited a small number of redactions where reference to officials was made. In each case we found that either the redaction was unnecessary, or the event in question had limited significance to the thrust of the report, or the reference to officials could have been retained with dexterous editing of the paragraph in question. We do not believe, however, that a charge of cover-up by the author or the Safeguarding Board can be justified.

7.66   The principle that the child's welfare must be the paramount consideration is explicitly stated in Government guidance[17] and this should inform all future debate and policy on redactions.

---

[17] 'Working Together to Safeguard Children (March 2012)

8. The response of other services and agencies

This chapter concentrates on the response to CSE from agencies including the Police, schools, taxis and licensing, Health and the Crown Prosecution Service. Historic policing issues are dealt with throughout the report. We acknowledge the priority given by the Police at the present time to protecting child victims and taking action against the perpetrators. It was not within the scope of the Inquiry to conduct in depth investigations into these service areas, but we are able to make some observations based on the evidence obtained. In some instances, the content is mainly descriptive, due to the limited amount of historic information available, and the absence of reference to CSE, as opposed to child protection, in records and files.

South Yorkshire Police

8.1   We deal with the response of South Yorkshire Police at some length throughout this report.   While there was close liaison between the Police, Risky Business and children's social care from the early days of the Risky Business project, there were very many historic cases where the operational response of the Police fell far short of what could be expected. The reasons for this are not entirely clear. The Police had excellent procedures from 1998, but in practice these appear to have been widely disregarded. Certainly there is evidence that police officers on the ground in the 1990s and well beyond displayed attitudes that conveyed a lack of understanding of the problem of CSE and the nature of grooming. We have already seen that children as young as 11 were deemed to be having consensual sexual intercourse when in fact they were being raped and abused by adults.

8.2   We were contacted by someone who worked at the Rotherham interchange in the early 2000s. He described how the Police refused to intervene when young girls who were thought to be victims of CSE were being beaten up and abused by perpetrators. According to him, the attitude of the Police at that time seemed to be that they were all 'undesirables' and the young women were not worthy of police protection.

8.3   By 2007, there was evidence that the Police were more pro-active in tackling CSE. Senior police officers had established good liaison arrangements with Risky Business and progress was being made in protecting the children and investigating the perpetrators.

8.4   The Police were commended by the trial judge, along with children's social care, for their handling of a successful prosecution in 2007. Shortly thereafter, work began on what would eventually lead to the successful prosecution of five offenders in 2009 as part of Operation Central, brought about by excellent joint working between the Police, Risky Business and children's social care.

8.5   We interviewed many serving police officers at different levels of seniority during the fieldwork for the Inquiry. It was clear that tackling child sexual exploitation was now a priority for South Yorkshire Police and we describe elsewhere their contribution to the inter-agency response.

8.6 There were a number of recent and on-going police operations to investigate and prosecute perpetrators of CSE. Some of these were run jointly with children's social care. They included investigations into historic abuse cases, one a Rotherham investigation and a second a Yorkshire-wide operation. There have been recent operations to target suspect hotels and limousine companies and an operation was underway looking at high-risk missing children. Joint training of hotel managers had resulted in one perpetrator being caught with two under-age girls.

8.7 A police analyst is now based in Rotherham, and produces a well presented monthly report on CSE. This provides detailed information about progress under the strategic objectives for CSE – Prevent, Protect and Pursue. This has greatly improved the quality of the information the CSE sub-group receives for monitoring purposes.

8.8 We considered that the Police were now appropriately resourced to deal with child sexual exploitation and had a clear focus on prevention, protection, investigating and prosecuting the perpetrators. We also found that police officers on the ground had a good child-centred focus and demonstrated a commitment to continuous improvement. Senior police officers were keen to develop the joint CSE team and were supportive of a single management arrangement similar to what is in place in Sheffield. They considered that this would strengthen the operation of the team.

Schools

8.9 Schools were a key element in the frontline of protecting children from sexual exploitation. Perpetrators targeted schools and there was evidence in the files (historically and up to the time of the Inquiry) that schools were proactive in alerting Risky Business, children's social care and the Police to signs and evidence of exploitation.

8.10 From its inception, Risky Business provided training programmes to schools with a view to raising young people's awareness of CSE and its dangers and giving them a chance to voice concerns about their own situation. Workshops in schools covered grooming and the internet. These programmes were maintained throughout the 2000s. By 2009 it was said that the demand for training on the part of schools was increasing markedly, although funding was a constraint for some. In 2012, the CSE team was working with 14 secondary schools. In the following year, the Safeguarding Board was told that exemplary work had been done with schools regarding CSE and that all schools, including faith schools, were signed up to the training.

8.11 Throughout this period, there were close working relationships between Risky Business and the Education Welfare Service. For example, in 2005 the Service was working with six girls who had been referred by Risky Business, and it had identified 18 girls for referral to Risky Business on account of concerns about sexual exploitation. The work of the Education Welfare Service in identifying young people at risk was commended by the Safeguarding Board in December 2012.

8.12   In December 2009, the Safeguarding Board received a policy paper 'Safeguarding Children Guidance for Madrassahs, Mosques and Supplementary Schools', which extended the scope of training and awareness-raising still further. There was also regular discussion of Children Missing from Education, in which the Education and Health services were working closely to locate missing children and to reduce the risks to which they might be exposed. In 2011, the effects of EU migration on school admissions and referrals to children's social care were reported to the Safeguarding Board. The number of Roma people in Rotherham was steadily increasing, as were concerns about child protection and child sexual exploitation within this group.

8.13   The young people we met in the course of the Inquiry were scathing about the sex education they received at school. They complained that it only focused on contraception. Some who had experienced Risky Business awareness-raising about CSE thought it was very good, particularly when a survivor spoke to them about her experience. They thought the sex education was out of touch and needed to be updated.

8.14   It is only recently that schools have been directly represented as members of the Safeguarding Board. In earlier years their interests were represented by senior officers of the Council, but they participated in sub-groups. Some found it difficult to attend, and this became an issue along with failure of some schools to complete Section 11 audits.

8.15   The report of the unannounced inspection by Ofsted in 2013 praised the advice given by schools and children's centres in relation to child protection. Many schools had a Child Exploitation and Online Protection Co-ordinator working with staff, parents and carers, and the largest proportion of referrals to the sexual exploitation team came from schools.

Taxis and Licensing

8.16   One of the common threads running through child sexual exploitation across England has been the prominent role of taxi drivers in being directly linked to children who were abused. This was the case in Rotherham from a very early stage, when residential care home heads met in the nineties to share intelligence about taxis and other cars which picked up girls from outside their units. In the early 2000s some secondary school heads were reporting girls being picked up at lunchtime at the school gates and being taken away to provide oral sex to men in the lunch break.

8.17   A diagram and backing papers supplied to the Police in 2001 by Risky Business linked alleged perpetrators with victims, taxi companies and individual drivers.

8.18   In the Borough at present there are 1200-1300 licensed taxi drivers, though they may not all be active. There are also well over 100 licensed taxi operators. The licensing of the vehicles and drivers is the responsibility of the local authority. There are statutory tests that must be complied with before a driver licence may be granted. The primary concern is for the 'fit and proper' test of the individual, although there is no legal definition of what this means. In Rotherham, applicants are obliged to obtain an enhanced disclosure from the Disclosure and Barring Service (DBS). The DBS check uses the same Police National Computer (PNC) information as the standard check but also includes a check of police intelligence records held locally. Any information held locally can at the discretion of the Chief Officer of Police be disclosed on the certificate.

8.19   The occupation of 'taxi driver' is a notifiable occupation. If a taxi driver is arrested or charged or convicted or is the subject of an investigation then the Licensing Authority is informed. The Licensing Authority may immediately suspend or revoke the licence if it is in the interests of public safety to do so. In 2010, the Council decided to locate all matters of temporary suspension with the relevant director, rather than with a less senior member of staff.

8.20   The Responsible Authorities' meetings in Rotherham were introduced in 2006 to share and discuss matters in relation to licensed premises such as late night takeaways, but they were later extended to include other matters related to licensing such as taxi and private hire licensing and safeguarding issues. Taxis are a standing item on the meeting's agenda. They are now held once every eight weeks with members including the Police, Fire, Child Safeguarding, Public Health and others. In March 2005, the Council's Task and Finish Group on CSE asked that discussions take place about safe travel, though there is no record of what specific actions followed. In June 2008 the Safeguarding Board learned that work had started involving taxi drivers and licensed premises as part of the preventive agenda by encouraging recognition and referral of young people thought to be at risk of sexual exploitation.

8.21   The Safeguarding Unit convened Strategy meetings from time to time on allegations involving taxi drivers. We read some of the most serious, from 2010, and were struck by the sense of exasperation, even hopelessness, recorded as the professionals in attendance tried to find ways of disrupting the suspected activity. Strategy meetings about one specific taxi firm had been held on four occasions in a seven week period. The minutes of one meeting record a total of ten girls and young women, three of whom were involved in three separate incidents of alleged attempted abduction by taxi drivers. The seven other girls had alleged that they were being sexually exploited in exchange for free taxi rides and goods. Two of the girls involved were looked after children. The Licensing Enforcement Officer took the step of formally writing to the Police following the incidents of alleged attempted abductions by drivers, complaining about the Police failure to act. In one incident, a driver accosted a 13-year-old girl. She refused to do what he asked and reported this to her parents who followed the taxi through the town, where they managed to identify the driver and dialled 999 for assistance. According to the Licensing Enforcement Officer, the Police did not attend until later and took no action. In his email to the Police he stated that 'a simple check would have revealed that the driver had been arrested a week previously in Bradford for a successful kidnapping of a lone female.' He concluded by acknowledging that police priorities were not the same as Licensing, but he 'should not be holding this together on his own'.

8.22 A further issue of safeguarding concerned those taxi firms which had a contract with the Council to transport some of the most vulnerable children to various resources within the authority. Some of the Council's difficulty was that they did not always have the drivers' names when allegations were made. Nor did they have a list of the drivers who transported children as part of the Council contract.

8.23 Following a review undertaken in 2012, the Council's Housing and Neighbourhood Services developed a formal procedure for the referral and communication of concerns about the safeguarding of children and vulnerable adults. This replaced a more informal arrangement. A plan for child safeguarding training for taxi drivers has also been put together with Sheffield City Council. Once finalised, it is intended that the training package will be delivered to all new applicants in Rotherham. This will be mandatory as part of the application process, and the existing drivers will be targeted in a phased way. The Council has also produced a 'Taxi Driver's Handbook', which includes CSE and safeguarding issues.

8.24 We were advised that four CSE related cases of taxi drivers had resulted in revocation of licence since 2009. They worked for four different companies. In one instance, the driver was arrested for sexual offences and supplying a controlled drug to a 15 year old girl. The CPS decided not to charge him, due to the perceived unreliability of one of the prosecution witnesses and the driver requested that the immediate suspension of his licence be lifted. However, the Licensing Board fully revoked the suspended driver licence. Council licensing staff described their relations with the taxi trade as being 'very difficult' on occasions, but they had always taken the right course of action on safeguarding issues. They worked closely with the Police, mostly on 'soft' intelligence, since written information tended to be much blander.

8.25 In a number of different meetings, the Inquiry talked to 24 young people, aged 14-25, who lived in the Council area. One of the main items for discussion with them was safe transport. When asked about taxis, there was an immediate and consistent response from the young women and men on every occasion. All avoided the use of taxis if at all possible. Their parents and partners strongly discouraged, even forbade, them from being on their own at night in a taxi, unless it was a company they personally knew. The girls described how on occasions they would be taken on the longest, darkest route home. One said the driver's first question would be 'How old are you, love?'. All talked about the content of their conversation quickly turning flirtatious or suggestive, including references to sex.

8.26 All the young people we met preferred to use the bus, despite their nervousness and dislike of the Rotherham Interchange, which they described as attracting drug dealers, addicts and people involved in a range of criminal activity. Many of these people congregated outside the Bus Station. The young people described their sense of intimidation and 'running the gauntlet' to get to their buses.

8.27 The use of limousines for purposes of sexual exploitation was raised by a number of people as a historic and current issue. It was also discussed at the Safeguarding Board in 2011. Such vehicles with more than 8 seats are nationally regulated by the Driver and Vehicle Standards Agency. In Rotherham, they have recently been seen waiting for young girls outside school gates. The Police have targeted limousine companies as part of organised operations to prevent sexual exploitation.

Crown Prosecution Service

8.28 It has not proved possible to follow up any individual cases where there were references to the Crown Prosecution Service in files and minutes dating back to 1997. We were told that those in the CPS before 2010 who would have dealt with CSE had all retired. For much of the period under review, the Police would cite the requirements of the CPS and their unwillingness to charge alleged perpetrators as the main reason so few prosecutions were pursued. In 2003, an SSI inspection noted that when Police had investigated and referred a case to the CPS, it had taken them nine months to decide not to proceed with the case.

8.29 The Crown Prosecution Service has recently undergone some internal reorganisation, which means that the CPS in Sheffield no longer deals with serious sexual offences, including CSE. A unit in Leeds and one in Hull now cover the South Yorkshire Police area.

8.30 Within the Safeguarding Board minutes, there was rarely reference to the CPS. It was noted in September 2011 that in relation to Operation Chard, it would be useful to know how the CPS had reached its conclusion on the case. The Board subsequently invited a representative from the CPS to discuss Operation Chard.

8.31 In June 2013, it was noted by the Safeguarding Board that they had sought representation from the CPS to serve on the CSE sub-group. By the end of 2013, no representative had been secured.

8.32 Senior police officers reported that the CPS had been much more helpful in CSE cases in their recent experience.

8.33 There are many issues that have been raised in other reports about the protection and support of child witnesses. These will be addressed in the new national policy and guidance for Police and the Crown Prosecution Service that will be drawn up by the College of Policing. It will include a checklist of support services that a victim of CSE ought to be offered following the decision to prosecute the case. It has been proposed elsewhere that this checklist should include, at the very least, pre-trial therapy, a pre-court familiarisation visit and a chance to meet the prosecuting barrister. In addition, all victims of CSE should be offered the services of an Independent Sexual Violence Adviser who is trained in court processes and, wherever possible, the same person should support the victim throughout the trial.

8.34   One survivor told us that victims who were witnesses needed much more support to help them through the whole process from the beginning. For some, it could be the fourth or fifth time they had been involved as witnesses. Very little was offered by way of support after a trial.

8.35   The Home Affairs Select Committee proposed that the CPS should review all prosecutions in CSE to identify barriers to taking cases forward, and outline best practice in supporting victims. It also recommended that the CPS should review recent cases to identify the key factors that led to successful prosecution.

8.36   In October 2013, the Director of Public Prosecutions at that time, Keir Starmer, revised the CPS guidance on child sexual exploitation to set out a clear, agreed approach which prosecutors would take to tackle cases of child sexual abuse. A list of stereotypical behaviours previously thought to undermine the credibility of young victims was included to dispel the associated myths when bringing a prosecution. These included:

- The victim invited sex by the way they dressed or acted
- The victim used alcohol or drugs and was therefore sexually available
- The victim didn't scream, fight or protest so they must have been consenting
- The victim didn't complain immediately, so it can't have been a sexual assault
- The victim is in a relationship with the alleged offender and is therefore a willing partner
- A victim should remember events consistently
- Children can consent to their own sexual exploitation
- CSE is only a problem in certain ethnic/cultural communities
- Only girls and young women are victims of child sexual abuse
- Children from BME backgrounds are not abused
- There will be physical evidence of abuse.

8.37   All of the above elements have been referred to at some point in historic files we read, usually as reasons given by the Police or the CPS for not pursuing suspected perpetrators. This guidance was welcomed by many of the main organisations, both statutory and voluntary, dealing with CSE.

Health

8.38 Effective partnership working with health was a key priority for the Local Safeguarding Board, as it was for its predecessor, the Area Child Protection Committee. Over the past ten years, the health service had been well represented at meetings of the Safeguarding Board by the hospital services, the Primary Care Trust, the Director of Nursing, the Director of Public Health and the Nurse Consultant on Safeguarding Children, amongst others. Strategic planning on CSE from a health perspective has been difficult to glean from historical records in the early part of the Inquiry period, although evident from individual files.

8.39 In the early 2000s, the Rotherham Health Professionals Child Protection Forum was established. In late 2005 an audit was conducted into the referrals made by health services to the children's social care Front Desk. It was found that the quality of referrals made by health visitors and other professionals was poor, but the response of children's social care was little better.

8.40 The Children First review of Children's Services in 2009 found that partnership working with NHS Rotherham had been well developed and represented 'highly advanced and ambitious practice'. It paid tribute to the leadership provided by the then chief executives of the two organisations, and to the ambition to create an integrated locality structure. However, implementation had proved difficult and the vision needed to be 'refreshed'. Aspects of the integrated locality model were later reversed. This is referred to in more detail in Chapter 13.

8.41 In November 2013, the Children, Young People and Families Partnership was advised of progress made in creating care pathways and safeguarding reporting mechanisms for young people accessing sexual health services in Rotherham. Protocols in relation to under-16 children attending the Genito-Urinary Medicine (GUM) and Contraceptive and Sexual Health (CaSH) clinics already included screening for sexual exploitation. These would be developed to raise the profile of CSE and to capture concerns about possible sexual exploitation, as well as 'algorithms' for referral to the newly appointed sexual exploitation nurse.

8.42 The Service Manager responsible for the CSE team told us that the appointment of the nurse to the team is one of the most positive initiatives in recent years, and gave examples of how this has speeded up children's access to appropriate health care.

8.43 The Inquiry interviewed the Director of Public Health, who had lengthy experience of both the Safeguarding Board and the Area Child Protection Committee. In his view, earlier meetings showed that there was general awareness of sexual abuse rather than sexual exploitation, and that sexual abuse was associated with individual perpetrators rather than with groups. In his opinion, physical abuse seemed to take higher priority. Awareness of sexual exploitation, especially in relation to the older age group of girls, came later towards the end of the decade. It had taken some time for the girls involved to be recognised as victims, and the justice system had some way to go in ensuring support and protection for victims and witnesses. He thought there had been a marked improvement over the past two or three years, with earlier intervention, better conducted risk assessments and agencies working more closely together, as epitomised by the interdisciplinary CSE team.

8.44 A number of those interviewed, including health professionals, commented on the complexity of the current health structure and its implications for accountability. There are several 'health organisations' within the NHS, who are represented at the Safeguarding Board and in other multi agency forums. These included Clinical Commissioning Groups, NHS (England), the Rotherham Hospital Trust, the RDASH Mental Health Trust, as well as the Director of Public Health located within the Council, and Public Health (England). This made it difficult to establish a single point of contact or a single representative, who could report back and consult with other parts of the service. Similarly, commissioning new services was complicated by the fragmentation of the various health bodies.

8.45 Both the Director of Public Health and two NHS Rotherham staff thought that local agencies should provide more consistent and longer term counselling and other supports to victims of sexual exploitation.

9. The Risky Business Project

The Risky Business project was the first public service in Rotherham to identify and support young people involved in child sexual exploitation. It operated on an outreach basis, working with large numbers of victims, as well as those at risk. The Council is to be commended for its financial commitment to the project and its work for most of its existence. From 2007, the project worked effectively with the Police on Operation Central. But it was too often seen as something of a nuisance, particularly by children's social care and there were many tensions between the two. There were allegations of exaggeration and unprofessional approaches by the project, none of which have been substantiated by this Inquiry. Management failed to address these problems and to enforce proper joint working and effective co-ordination so that the most was made of their distinctive contributions. The Risky Business project was incorporated within Safeguarding from 2011 and subsequently became part of the co-located joint CSE team in 2012.

9.1   Risky Business was a small team of youth workers, set up in 1997, following concerns by local staff about young people being abused through prostitution. After the project was established, a CSE inter-agency network was developed by voluntary and statutory agencies. In 1998, a small survey distributed by this network, identified 70 young women and 11 young men under 18 who were involved in exploitation, or prostitution as it was then termed. Area Child Protection Committee protocols were drafted and two regular meetings were established, which were later merged into a group known as 'Key Players'. ACPC training on sexual exploitation was first delivered following the launch of the procedures in November 2000. Risky Business contributed to all of these initiatives.

9.2   The Risky Business project aimed to provide support to young people in Rotherham, aged between 11 and 25 years, with two main purposes:

   a) To offer advice and information to young people in relation to sexual health, accommodation, drugs and alcohol, parenting and budgeting, eating disorder, self-harm and abuse; and to promote their self-esteem and self-assertiveness.

   b) To offer training in sexual exploitation, abuse and related matters to schools and to agencies and individuals working with young people.

9.3   For some years after its foundation, the funding of Risky Business was uncertain, though eventually the Council acknowledged its important work and increased its core budget.

9.4   Risky Business adopted an outreach approach, based on community development principles. That is, it started where the young person was; it concerned itself with the whole person and addressed any issues that the young person brought to the relationship; it did not prescribe or direct. Its methods were complementary to those of the statutory services. Its success depended upon the skills of the individual worker and the level of trust which young people were willing to commit to it. Its operations could be volatile, unpredictable, and even 'risky'. Nevertheless, it was performing a function which services with statutory responsibilities could not fully replicate. Any semblance of the statutory worker had to be set aside in order to create and retain trust.

9.5   In a report in 2008 on the Protection of Young People in Rotherham from Sexual Exploitation, it was stated that Risky Business 'continues to be the main service available to young people. It takes referrals, undertakes assessments of risk and directly intervenes to manage and reduce risk by working with young people and other agencies to devise and deliver exit plans'.

9.6   The key role played by Risky Business in the success of Operation Central was acknowledged by many, including the Police. The 'Lessons Learned' independent review (2010) reflected that its work was highly thought of by the young victims, and that it had good working relations with the Police. It even proposed a greater role for the project in ensuring that necessary actions were carried out in a way acceptable to victims. Recognising the value of the soft intelligence held by Risky Business, the District Commander (2006 - 2010) arranged for the project staff to be given training in intelligence gathering.

9.7   The Council also placed high value on the training programmes which Risky Business provided to schools, seeking to raise young people's awareness of sexual exploitation and its dangers; and it encouraged the extension of these programmes to a wide range of groups, formal and informal, within the community. The presentations on sexual exploitation that were given to councillors and senior officials in 2004-5 derived mainly from the work of Risky Business.

9.8   From an early stage, problems arose in the relationship between Risky Business and children's social care, particularly with regard to individual young people whose needs were thought by Risky Business to fall within the remit of the statutory services. It was essential that the relationship be built on mutual understanding and the preservation of the strengths of each. There would always be the inherent difficulty of transferring a young person from a non-statutory to a statutory service; of achieving the transition to the status of 'client', particularly if the young person regarded social workers with apprehension.

9.9   The task of dealing with issues between Risky Business and children's social care lay with management. Given the subsequent histories of some of the young people who were affected, it is tragic that in so many instances management failed to do so. There were too many examples of young people who were properly referred by Risky Business to children's social care and who somehow fell through the net and were not treated with the priority that they deserved. It is almost as if the source of the referral from Risky Business was a pretext for attaching lower importance to it.

9.10   Interviews with managers in post at that time (around mid 2000s) confirm this view. 'They were regarded as a group of youth workers who were treading on their territory' said one. Another senior manager 'disbelieved' what Risky Business presented, describing it as almost 'professional gossip'. Tensions manifested themselves in a number of ways, and particularly in individual cases. All agreed that relationships were not good between the project and children's social care. Managers of children's social care wished to bring the project firmly into a child protection approach, whilst project staff wanted to advocate on behalf of the girls involved and protect their confidentiality.

9.11   Children's social care would complain that the referral was not accompanied by the detailed information, which was necessary for its acceptance. Serious criticism of the Risky Business record keeping is referred to elsewhere in this report, in particular in the findings of the Child S Serious Case Review. Having read a sample of the Risky Business records, this inquiry did not find these criticisms justified. Where records were available, they were detailed and well kept. They were judged to be equivalent to the standard of many of the contemporaneous children's social care records on children in need. Child protection and looked after children files were of a higher standard.

9.12   Several people interviewed were of the view that the project's success, particularly in Operation Central, was one of the causes of professional jealousy, which led to them being assigned a lesser role in Operation Czar and for children's social care staff to take the lead with the individual girls involved. This proved to be a serious misjudgement, as is referred to in Chapter 13.

9.13   It is not the intention of this overview to overstate the achievements of Risky Business. Its staff readily acknowledge that they made mistakes and that their enthusiasm and frustration may sometimes have led them into breaking rules and frequently getting into trouble. There were periods when relationships between Risky Business and the statutory agencies were poor, and a less confrontational approach might have strengthened joint working. A senior person from another local voluntary organisation commented that single-issue projects always faced the risk of focusing on their own issue to the exclusion of others. However, for many years Risky Business was the only service within the Council to consistently recognise the gravity of child sexual exploitation in the Borough and the severe damage that it was causing to young people. By its nature, the project's style made a bad fit with the more structured services involved. The failure of management to understand and resolve this problem has been a running flaw in the development of child protection services relating to sexual exploitation in Rotherham.

9.14   The project has now been incorporated within the joint CSE team. It is doubtful whether its original ethos and style of working can survive this absorption into the statutory system, where it is firmly located in a child protection model. The grounds for the move included the belief that Risky Business lacked managerial and risk assessment skills, the rigour of case management supervision, procedures, risk management plans, defined roles and responsibilities, and office systems. All of which fails to recognise the quality of their work with individual children, and their distinctively different professional role, and entirely misses the point.

10. Three Early Reports

A chapter of a draft report on research into CSE in Rotherham, often referred to as 'The Home Office Report', was written by a researcher in 2002. It contained severe criticisms of the agencies in Rotherham involved with CSE. The most serious concerned alleged indifference towards, and ignorance of, child sexual exploitation on the part of senior managers. The report also stated that responsibility was continuously placed on young people's shoulders, rather than with the suspected abusers. It presented a clear picture of a 'high prevalence of young women being coerced and abused through prostitution.' Senior officers in the Police and the Council were deeply unhappy about the data and evidence that underpinned the report. There was a suggestion that facts had been fabricated or exaggerated. Several sources reported that the researcher was subjected to personalised hostility at the hands of officials. She was unable to complete the last part of the research. The content which senior officers objected to has been shown with hindsight to be largely accurate. Had this report been treated with the seriousness it merited at the time by both the Police and the Council, the children involved then and later would have been better protected and abusers brought to justice. These events have led to suspicions of collusion and cover up.

Dr Heal's reports present a vivid and alarming picture of the links between sexual exploitation, drugs, gangs and violent crime in Rotherham from 2002 to 2006. They were widely distributed to middle and senior managers in all key agencies. There is no record of any formal, specific discussion of these reports in Council papers, in ACPC minutes or in the Rotherham Safeguarding Children Board minutes made available to the Inquiry.

10.1   The reports covered in this chapter indicate the extent of knowledge and research about CSE in Rotherham which was available to the agencies involved during the earlier part of the Inquiry period.

The Home Office Research

10.2   The Home Office Crime Reduction Programme (CRP) initiated a number of research projects throughout England in 2001, aimed at providing an evidence base on tackling street prostitution. They reviewed services that were working to protect young people at risk or actively involved in prostitution. Three projects in Bristol, Sheffield and Rotherham, made up the 'young people and prostitution' part of the research. Each of the three had its own focus. The Rotherham focus was on perpetrators. This required a significant amount of 'profiling' to be done. It also drew heavily on ten case studies of known victims in the town. The Rotherham research was based on Risky Business, and the researcher was appointed by the Council on behalf of the local partners and was based in Council premises.

10.3   The Bristol and Sheffield projects were funded from January 2001 until March 2003, and the Rotherham project from January 2001 until July 2002. The final report on the research from the Home Office included a footnote, stating that Rotherham was not funded for the second year due to 'implementation problems'. The University of Luton's final evaluation report did not include the Rotherham project.

10.4   A document headed 'Chapter Four: Key Achievements of the Home Office Pilot' was made available to the Inquiry by the Council. It referred to the evaluation results of the pilot in Rotherham, though the town is not named. It provided a descriptive background to CSE within the town going back to 1996, drawing on the work of Risky Business, which is referred to in the report as 'the project'. The rest of the report containing the overview of the aims and objectives of the pilot, literature review, methodology and recommendations, is missing.

10.5   The report was not dated but we understand that it was written in 2002.

10.6   The present Chief Executive and Executive Director of Children's Services saw the report referred to below for the first time in 2012.

10.7   The report gave due credit to good practice where it occurred and noted improvements which had taken place over the period of the research. These included:

a) the raised profile of abuse through prostitution;

b) the revision of the Missing Persons procedure;

c) the post of Sexual Exploitation Co-ordinator was created (though unclear whether it was ever filled);

d) the Keepsafe project was a valuable initiative;

e) more inter-agency meetings were held to share concerns about young people affected by exploitation;

f) methods of recording CSE were improved;

g) CSE became a key objective for the ACPC for 2002-2003; and

h) Multi-agency training was provided to a wide range of agencies, but was not taken up by the Police or local magistrates.

10.8   The examples of poor practice and negative attitudes were far more prevalent. These included:

a) Awareness of CSE and interest in it were not widespread. Effective interventions were lacking;

b) Some professionals were working as individuals rather than seeking inter-agency solutions;

c) Information was not being shared with the Police, and Strategy meetings were not being called by children's social care;

d) The 'mapping exercise' devised by Risky Business that cross-referenced a large amount of data on victims and perpetrators was not well received by the Police. No charges were brought against alleged perpetrators, nor was any investigation undertaken.

e) The Police had responded reluctantly to missing person reports, as a 'waste of time'. Some young women had been threatened with arrest for wasting police time;

f) The young women concerned were often seen by the Police as being deviant or promiscuous. The adult men with whom they were found were not questioned;

g) A database was developed to provide consistent recording of CSE-related information across agencies. Owing to a dispute between these agencies, it was not used;

h) Possibly as a result of their experience, parents were often not reporting a missing child since they saw it as a waste of time;

i) Professionals were reluctant to be named as a source of information in prosecution, fearing for their safety. Some Police said that if young people were not prepared to help themselves by making complaints against their abusers and giving evidence, they would take no further action on the case;

j) Despite ACPC procedures, there was no consistent way of addressing the issue of CSE. Many professionals were unaware of it; and

k) Some professionals were cautious about working together and sharing information. Some feared an increase in workload. Some, especially the Police, made personal judgements about the young women involved.

10.9 According to the researcher, attempts to raise many of the concerns described above with senior personnel were met with defensiveness and hostility.

10.10 The researcher gave the Inquiry an account of her mounting frustration and concern at the lack of action to pursue the perpetrators, despite monthly meetings with the Police at which the project provided intelligence about the men concerned. She also had concerns regarding the lack of action taken to protect young people at risk and was conscious that the end of the pilot was in sight, with no positive progress in these areas. There were continuing incidents of serious abuse being perpetrated against vulnerable children.

10.11 She described a particular case that was 'the final straw'. [18] In 2001, a young girl who had been repeatedly raped had tried to escape her perpetrators but was terrified of reprisals. They had allegedly put all the windows in at the parental home and broken both of her brother's legs 'to send a message'. At that point, the child agreed to make a complaint to the Police. The researcher took her to the police station office where she would be interviewed in advance in order to familiarise her with the place and the officer who would be conducting the interview. Whilst there, the girl received a text from the main perpetrator. He had with him her 11-year old sister. He said repeatedly to her 'your choice...'. The girl did not proceed with the complaint. She disengaged from the pilot and project and is quoted by the researcher as saying 'you can't protect me'. This incident raised questions about how the perpetrator knew

---

[18] This case is also mentioned in Chapter 5. It was one of the case files read independently by the Inquiry team, and the details given by the researcher were found to be accurate.

where the young woman was and what she was doing.

10.12 Following this incident, the researcher described how she discussed what to do next with her manager and others in the project and pilot's Steering Committee. It was agreed that she should put her concerns in writing to the Chief Constable of South Yorkshire Police and the Rotherham District Commander of Police. This letter was approved by her manager and the steering group before being hand-delivered to Rotherham Police Station. The Inquiry had access to this letter. According to the researcher, this resulted in a meeting with the District Commander and senior Council officials at which she was instructed never to do such a thing again. The content of her letter was not discussed.

10.13 Prior to completion of the draft report, the researcher had to submit her data to the Home Office. When senior Council and police officers saw it, the Council suspended the researcher on the basis that she had committed 'an act of gross misconduct' by including in the data minutes of confidential inter-agency meetings. A formal meeting took place the following week at which the researcher was reinstated after she was able to show that the minutes had in fact been handed to the Home Office evaluators by her manager. It was agreed that she would receive a positive reference from the Council when her temporary contract terminated. The Council also paid for counselling. She spent the remainder of her time working on policies and procedures, in a room on her own, forbidden access to the girls involved and not allowed to attend meetings or have access to further data.

10.14 According to the researcher, a request, made via her manager, from senior council officials and the District Commander was that she edit the data sent to the Home Office evaluator, and remove or rewrite several sections that they judged to be inaccurate or exaggerated. The District Commander had a different recollection, namely that at the time she suggested editing out any identifying information about the children involved before the report was circulated to other agencies. The Inquiry had access to copies of the researcher's case studies. These were all appropriately anonymised to protect the identity of the victims.

10.15 The researcher told the Inquiry that she verified the accuracy of her findings and sent the report including the Chapter 4 referred to above, to the Home Office evaluators and senior officials on the last day of her employment, without incorporating any of the changes proposed by the officers concerned. Funding for the second year of the pilot was withheld by the Home Office and Rotherham was excluded from the final research report because of "implementation problems".

10.16 The District Commander of Police (2001-2005) remembered the 'Home Office' report, and its criticisms of the Police, but recalled nothing of any 'row' surrounding it, nor anything to do with action taken against the researcher. The Head of Function for Safeguarding at the time and several others, including the Chief Executive (see Chapter 11), recalled the Police and senior Council officers as being very angry about it.

10.17   The researcher's line-manager, who chaired the meeting to discuss the alleged gross misconduct thought the whole incident had been badly handled and the researcher had been very badly treated. She confirmed that there was a great deal of personal hostility and anger towards the researcher and her work on the part of senior people.

10.18   Much of what was contained in this report, and in particular the criticisms and concerns of the research officer, has been confirmed by the Inquiry from other sources. The Inquiry case-file reading exercise covered six out of those ten cases that formed her case studies. Apart from a very small number of minor details (e.g. a slight variation in the date of an event), we found the cases studies to be entirely consistent with our own reading of the files, and we considered them to evidence a high standard of professional judgement and accuracy. The secrecy around this report, the discrepancies in the accounts we received from senior people and the treatment of the researcher were all deeply troubling to the Inquiry team. They have inevitably led to suspicion of collusion and intended cover-up. If the senior people concerned had paid more attention to the content of the report, more might have been done to help children who were being violently exploited and abused.

Reports by Dr Angie Heal, Strategic Drugs Analyst

a)   **Sexual Exploitation, Drug Use and Drug Dealing: Current Situation in South Yorkshire (2003)**

b)   **Violence and Gun Crime: Links with Sexual Exploitation, Prostitution and Drug Markets in South Yorkshire (2006).**

10.19   In 2002, South Yorkshire Police and their partners appointed Dr Angie Heal, a strategic drugs analyst, to carry out research on drug use, drug dealing and related problems in the county. She was based with South Yorkshire Police and did this research in the period 2002-2006. She produced several 'stand alone' reports, including the two referred to here, as well as six-monthly updates. The two reports had a similar format of looking at the overall position in South Yorkshire, as well as examining each of the four policing areas separately i.e. Rotherham, Doncaster, Barnsley and Sheffield.

10.20   As a minimum, these reports went to each South Yorkshire Police District Commander, Chief Superintendents and Superintendents in Specialist Crime Services (CID) and Community Safety. They also went to Drug Action Coordinators, NHS and voluntary sector drug agencies as well as organisations working with children and adults involved in exploitation and prostitution. They also went to the Central Government office for the North East. Latterly, they were also sent to the Partnership Police Inspectors who were attached to each local authority Community Safety Partnership, as well as the Principal Community Safety Officers in each of the local authorities in the county. It became clear to Dr Heal at an early stage that there were important links between drugs, drug dealing and child sexual exploitation, which she continued to highlight to her funding partners in her reports and updates throughout her employment as a researcher.

10.21 In November 2004, a presentation on sexual exploitation was made to the Rotherham Executive Group for Children and Young People's Services. According to Council papers, the information pack provided to those attending drew on Dr Heal's 2003 report, as well as two other relevant documents. The Inquiry asked the Council if the 2003 report had been considered by the Council, and the response was that no reference to the report could be found.

10.22 The main findings of the 2003 report were:

a) most of the men in South Yorkshire who were involved in the sexual exploitation of young people for the purposes of prostitution were also believed to be involved in drug dealing. They might also be involved in rape, violence, gun crime, robbery and other serious criminal offences;

b) Rotherham was described as not having a 'street scene' but there were a 'significant number of girls and some boys who are being sexually exploited';

c) Some of the young women who were being sexually exploited were subject to violence, rape, gang rape, kidnap, carrying drugs, dealing drugs, and found in situations where firearms were present;

d) Four brothers who had been targeting young women for their own and others' gratification were identified as the main focus of concern for Risky Business;

e) The Police recalled one 12-year old who described being taken to a hotel by some men and being made to watch while her 14-year old sister had sex with them. They spoke of another young girl who was doused in petrol as a threat against reporting sexual offences. Another 14-year old was selling drugs for one of the main perpetrators, who had been very violent towards her and her mother. This man's brother tried to strangle another young girl;

f) A significant number of the girls involved got pregnant; and

g) Anger, depression and acts of self-harm by the girls involved were evident in many from a very early stage.

10.23 The main findings of the 2006 report were:

a) The situation in 2006 in Rotherham was described as continuing 'as it has done for a number of years', with an established sexual exploitation scene which was very organised and involved systematic physical and sexual violence against young women;

b) It also involved young women being trafficked to other towns and cities predominantly in the north;

c) The level of intimidation, physical beatings and rape amongst exploited girls was considered by multi-agency staff to be very severe and their situation to be very serious. None of the perpetrators were believed to use substances which would contribute to such levels of violence;

d) It was reported that a number of workers in the town involved with the issue believed that one of the difficulties which prevented CSE being dealt with effectively was the ethnicity of the perpetrators;

e) The author emphasised the importance of the attitude taken to these crimes and to the victims, particularly by the Police and children's social care;

f) The most significant recent development had been a rise in reports of guns being seen rather than used by men involved in CSE in Rotherham and Sheffield; and

g) There had been a high-profile media campaign about the trafficking from Eastern Europe of young women and girls for the purposes of prostitution. Whilst laudable in itself, the abuse of local girls for the same purpose appeared to be largely ignored.

11.   Issues of ethnicity

Issues of ethnicity related to child sexual exploitation have been discussed in other reports, including the Home Affairs Select Committee report, and the report of the Children's Commissioner. Within the Council, we found no evidence of children's social care staff being influenced by concerns about the ethnic origins of suspected perpetrators when dealing with individual child protection cases, including CSE. In the broader organisational context, however, there was a widespread perception that messages conveyed by some senior people in the Council and also the Police, were to 'downplay' the ethnic dimensions of CSE. Unsurprisingly, frontline staff appeared to be confused as to what they were supposed to say and do and what would be interpreted as 'racist'. From a political perspective, the approach of avoiding public discussion of the issues was ill judged.

There was too much reliance by agencies on traditional community leaders such as elected members and imams as being the primary conduit of communication with the Pakistani-heritage community. The Inquiry spoke to several Pakistani-heritage women who felt disenfranchised by this and thought it was a barrier to people coming forward to talk about CSE. Others believed there was wholesale denial of the problem in the Pakistani-heritage community in the same way that other forms of abuse were ignored. Representatives of women's groups were frustrated that interpretations of the Borough's problems with CSE were often based on an assumption that similar abuse did not take place in their own community and therefore concentrated mainly on young white girls.

Both women and men from the community voiced strong concern that other than two meetings in 2011, there had been no direct engagement with them about CSE over the past 15 years, and this needed to be addressed urgently, rather than 'tiptoeing' around the issue.

Ethnic Minorities and Safeguarding Issues

11.1   Census information from 2011 showed that Rotherham had nearly 8000 people with Pakistani or Kashmiri ethnicity, or 3.1% of the Borough population, an increase from 2% in the previous census. 77% of this population lived in one of three central wards of Rotherham. There are eight mosques in Rotherham. There were few references in any minutes to ethnic minorities or migrant families until 2006, when concern was raised at the Safeguarding Board about the living conditions of migrant families. Young people were thought to be at risk of physical or sexual abuse for a variety of reasons. Some had been separated from their own families. There were also issues of poverty, forced marriage and child abduction. In the early months of 2005, twelve cases of forced marriage had been dealt with in Rotherham - the highest in the South Yorkshire Police area. Of particular concern was the young age of many of the girls involved.

11.2   As has been stated many times before, there is no simple link between race and child sexual exploitation, and across the UK the greatest numbers of perpetrators of CSE are white men. The second largest category, according to the Children's Commissioner's report, are those from a minority ethnic background, particularly those recorded as 'Asian'. In Rotherham, the majority of known perpetrators were of Pakistani heritage including the five men convicted in 2010. The file reading carried out by the Inquiry also confirmed that the ethnic origin of many perpetrators was 'Asian'. In one major case in the mid-2000s, the convicted perpetrator was Afghan. Latterly, some child victims of CSE and some perpetrators had originated from the Roma Slovak community, with a steady increase in the number of child protection cases involving Roma children, though mainly in the category of neglect. Work with Roma families was one of the six priorities of the Child Sexual Exploitation sub-group of the Safeguarding Board in 2012. The Roma population in Rotherham was proportionately much larger than in bigger areas such as Bradford and Manchester.

11.3   By March 2012, the child protection profile was showing that Rotherham had more than double the English average for Roma Slovak families being referred under Section 47 of the Children Act 1989.

The Early Years

11.4   Dr Heal, in her 2003 report, stated that 'In Rotherham the local Asian community are reported to rarely speak about them [the perpetrators].' The subject was taboo and local people were probably equally frightened of the violent tendencies of the perpetrators as the young women they were abusing. In her 2006 report she described how the appeal of organised sexual exploitation for Asian gangs had changed. In the past, it had been for their personal gratification, whereas now it offered 'career and financial opportunities to young Asian men who got involved'. She also noted that Iraqi Kurds and Kosovan men were participating in organised activities against young women.

11.5   In her 2006 report, she stated that 'it is believed by a number of workers that one of the difficulties that prevent this issue [CSE] being dealt with effectively is the ethnicity of the main perpetrators'.

11.6   She also reported in 2006 that young people in Rotherham believed at that time that the Police dared not act against Asian youths for fear of allegations of racism. This perception was echoed at the present time by some young people we met during the Inquiry, but was not supported by specific examples.

11.7   Several people interviewed expressed the general view that ethnic considerations had influenced the policy response of the Council and the Police, rather than in individual cases. One example was given by the Risky Business project Manager (1997- 2012) who reported that she was told not to refer to the ethnic origins of perpetrators when carrying out training. Other staff in children's social care said that when writing reports on CSE cases, they were advised by their managers to be cautious about referring to the ethnicity of the perpetrators.

Officer Involvement

11.8 All the senior officers we interviewed were asked whether ethnic considerations influenced their decision making. All were unequivocal that this did not happen. However, several of those involved in the operational management of services reported some attempts to pressurise them into changing their approach to some issues. This mainly affected the support given to Pakistani-heritage women fleeing domestic violence, where a small number of councillors had demanded that social workers reveal the whereabouts of these women or effect reconciliation rather than supporting the women to make up their own minds. The Inquiry team was confident that ethnic issues did not influence professional decision-making in individual cases.

11.9 Frontline staff did not report personal experience of attempts to influence their practice or decision making because of ethnic issues. Those who had involvement in CSE were acutely aware of these issues and recalled a general nervousness in the earlier years about discussing them, for fear of being thought racist.

11.10 Good work was done by officers in developing a protocol on child protection issues in the mosques in 2008. Each mosque appointed a designated person responsible for child protection, and training was provided for imams and others. The current chair of the Rotherham Council of Mosques had made strenuous efforts to widen representation on his Council to include women and demonstrated a strong personal commitment to dealing with child protection and CSE. He was disappointed not to have had any contact from the Safeguarding Board in the past, but was encouraged by recent discussions.

Political Engagement.

11.11 The issue of race, regardless of ethnic group, should be tackled as an absolute priority if it is known to be a significant factor in the criminal activity of organised abuse in any local community. There was little evidence of such action being taken in Rotherham in the earlier years. Councillors can play an effective role in this, especially those representing the communities in question, but only if they act as facilitators of communication rather than barriers to it. One senior officer suggested that some influential Pakistani-heritage councillors in Rotherham had acted as barriers.

11.12 Several councillors interviewed believed that by opening up these issues they could be 'giving oxygen' to racist perspectives that might in turn attract extremist political groups and threaten community cohesion. To some extent this concern was valid, with the apparent targeting of the town by groups such as the English Defence League. The Deputy Council Leader (2011-2014) from the Pakistani-heritage community was clear that he had not understood the scale of the CSE problem in Rotherham until 2013. He then disagreed with colleague elected members on the way to approach it. He had advocated taking the issue 'head on' but had been overruled. He was one of the elected members who said they thought the criminal convictions in 2010 were 'a one-off, isolated case', and not an example of a more deep-rooted problem of Pakistani-heritage perpetrators targeting young white girls. This was at best naïve, and at worst ignoring a politically inconvenient truth.

11.13 Both the Council and the Police used traditional channels of communication with the Pakistani-heritage community for many years on general issues of child protection. There seemed, from all accounts, to be very few, if any, specific discussions of CSE, though this was difficult to verify. These contacts were almost exclusively with men.

Pakistani-heritage Women and Girls

11.14 One of the local Pakistani women's groups described how Pakistani-heritage girls were targeted by taxi drivers and on occasion by older men lying in wait outside school gates at dinner times and after school. They also cited cases in Rotherham where Pakistani landlords had befriended Pakistani women and girls on their own for purposes of sex, then passed on their name to other men who had then contacted them for sex. The women and girls feared reporting such incidents to the Police because it would affect their future marriage prospects.

11.15 The UK Muslim Women's Network produced a report on CSE in September 2013 which drew on 35 case studies of women from across the UK who were victims, the majority of whom were Muslim. It highlighted that Asian girls were being sexually exploited where authorities were failing to identify or support them. They were most vulnerable to men from their own communities who manipulated cultural norms to prevent them from reporting their abuse. It described how this abuse was being carried out. 'Offending behaviour mostly involved men operating in groups . . . The victim was being passed around and prostituted amongst many other men. Our research also showed that complex grooming 'hierarchies' were at play. The physical abuse included oral, anal and vaginal rape; role play; insertion of objects into the vagina; severe beatings; burning with cigarettes; tying down; enacting rape that included ripping clothes off and sexual activity over the webcam.' This description mirrors the abuse committed by Pakistani-heritage perpetrators on white girls in Rotherham.

11.16 The Deputy Children's Commissioner's report reached a similar conclusion to the Muslim Women's Network research, stating 'one of these myths was that only white girls are victims of sexual exploitation by Asian or Muslim males, as if these men only abuse outside of their own community, driven by hatred and contempt for white females. This belief flies in the face of evidence that shows that those who violate children are most likely to target those who are closest to them and most easily accessible.' The Home Affairs Select Committee quoted witnesses saying that cases of Asian men grooming Asian girls did not come to light because victims 'are often alienated and ostracised by their own families and by the whole community, if they go public with allegations of abuse.'

11.17 With hindsight, it is clear that women and girls in the Pakistani community in Rotherham should have been encouraged and empowered by the authorities to speak out about perpetrators and their own experiences as victims of sexual exploitation, so often hidden from sight. The Safeguarding Board has recently received a presentation from a local Pakistani women's group about abuse within their community. The Board should address as a priority the under-reporting of exploitation and abuse in minority ethnic communities. We recommend that the relevant agencies immediately initiate dialogue about CSE with minority ethnic communities, and in particular with the Pakistani-heritage community. This should be done in consultation with local women's groups, and should develop strategies that support young women and girls from the community to participate without fear or threat.

12. Workforce Strategy and Financial Resources

From 2009, the Council achieved a significant reversal of its long-standing vacancy problems with the development of an effective workforce strategy. The Council was coping with severe cost pressures as a result of cutbacks and other changes to local authority funding. Despite this, it has protected expenditure on children's safeguarding and improved its position from the lowest spend per head to the average, when compared with its benchmarking partners. At the time of the Inquiry it was facing a very difficult budgetary position for the foreseeable future.

Recruitment, Retention and Workforce Development

12.1 From the early 2000s, Rotherham started to experience problems in the recruitment of social workers, whilst facing budgetary pressures, high levels of demand, and increasing complexity of work, including CSE. The Social Services Inspectorate commented in a 2003 report on the serious vacancy levels, and there were regular reports to the Lead Member on the impact on services of staff shortages. This became very acute in 2008-09.

12.2 The present Executive Director of Children's Services recalled that at the time of her appointment in 2008 the vacancy rate was at its worst at 43%. At the time of the Ofsted inspection in 2009, it was in excess of 37% of the establishment posts and more than one in every two team manager posts was also vacant. Both social worker and manager unfilled posts were covered by agency staff, with the additional expense and other difficulties this created. There is no doubt that these workforce problems lay at the core of the quality of practice issues judged to be 'inadequate' by Ofsted.

12.3 In parallel with this there was a shortage of experienced children and families' social workers in the wider marketplace. In Rotherham, in keeping with other councils, there was a stable group of social workers in specialist posts such as Fostering and Adoption, but a deficit in the frontline child protection and children in need posts.

12.4 The DfE set targets for Rotherham to reduce its vacancy rate to 15% or less by December 2010. The Council was successful in meeting these targets and for the last three years it has maintained a low vacancy rate. For 2013 this was 4%, against an all England average of 12%.

12.5 There were several elements to the development of the Council's successful workforce strategy. One has been the systematic strengthening of links with the local universities which train social workers, with specific targeting of children's social work in the provision of practice placements. This was in recognition of the fact that good local authority placements often lead newly qualifying workers to work for that authority. Social workers we spoke to commented that their lecturers at university recommended Rotherham very highly for placements because of the quality of experience they would receive.

12.6 Another important strand in the retention strategy was investment in intensive support of newly qualified social workers. This approach, entitled the Assessed and Supported Year in Employment, involves caseload protection and the use of Social Work Practice Consultants, who enhance the traditional line management supervision process. The feedback from social workers about this support was extremely positive.

12.7 A third element in the strategy was the Council's investment in Continuous Professional Development, which offered team managers sponsorship to undertake the University of Sheffield's MA in professional practice, as well as other personalised learning options, including Team Manager Learning Sets.

12.8 The Council deserves recognition for its successful 'turnaround' in vacancy rates, which has created a stable workforce and significantly reduced reliance on agency staff. This was due to a carefully planned and implemented workforce strategy. The social workers and team managers we met spoke highly of Rotherham as an employer, and especially about the learning and development opportunities they had. All would recommend it as a place to work.

Financial Resources

12.9 For the earlier years of the Inquiry, the department of social services had an integrated budget for children and adults. Few financial records were available, specifically about children's social care. However, other reports provide some relevant data.[19]

12.10 For the period 2000/01 to 2002/03:

a) the budget for children's social care, whilst increasing in cash terms, decreased in its proportion of the total budget for social services by 0.7 per cent;

b) in the same period the children's social care budget had been overspent by nearly a million pounds in two years. This was largely explained by unpredictable levels of expenditure on placements for children outside the Borough;

c) the Council had progressively increased its children's social care budget compared with the Standard Spending Assessment (SSA) but the percentage expenditure was still below the England average, placing Rotherham third lowest in its comparator group; and

d) gross expenditure on looked after children was just above the national average but the numbers of LAC were some 26% above the national average.

12.11 The SSI report from which the above data was drawn concluded that patterns of expenditure in children's social care did not promote preventive services.

12.12 Financial records available thereafter show that from 2005/2008:

---

[19] Social Services Inspectorate Report Feb 2003, & Rotherham data sources.

a) the Children and Young People 's Safeguarding budget performed more or less on target;

b) from then to 2012/13, there were overspends in every year;

c) savings taken from this line year on year were disproportionately lower than the percentage taken from other Council services, and investments in children's services were significantly higher; and

d) in the 2014/15 financial year there were no planned investments for any Council services.

12.13 The combined effect of changes to local authority funding in England has been a dramatic reduction in resources available to Rotherham and neighbouring Councils. By 2016, Rotherham will have lost 33% of its spending power in real terms compared to 2010/11. The comparison for the whole of England is a reduction of 20%, and for a Council like Buckinghamshire, only 4.5% reduction. These figures highlight the extreme pressure that reductions in public spending are placing on Councils such as Rotherham, which is faced with high demands for vulnerable children and families' services, associated with significant levels of poverty and deprivation.

12.14 The report commissioned by the Council and NHS Rotherham from Children First in 2009 considered the issue of Children's Services funding in some depth, drawing on 2008/09 data. Amongst it conclusions were:

a) the Council had invested considerably in school provision, health and foster care provision;

b) with the exception of adoption services, spending on children's social care was low;

c) spending on looked after children was especially low, possibly risky;

d) at the same time the activity levels for children's social care showed referrals to be very high, but accompanied by lower levels of assessments and reviews;

e) in comparison to the benchmarking group of authorities, expenditure on residential, fostering and family support services was in the lower quartile; and

f) the additional needs of Slovakian/Roma children and families should be reviewed each year.

12.15 The reports available to the Inquiry did not tell us how well senior managers quantified unmet need and its associated costs or whether this information was presented to members in each annual budget. It was therefore hard to determine if council members had a realistic understanding of the cost of meeting the needs of vulnerable children, the impact of rising demand, and the fact that funding in Rotherham was at a very low base.

12.16 The Executive Director of Children's Services (2008 to date) thought that in the past too much emphasis had been placed by senior safeguarding staff on financial resources being the solution to all of the service's problems, rather than also looking at what could be done to improve efficiency and practice. The Lead Member for

Children and Young People's Services (2005-2009) indicated he had become increasingly concerned about the underfunding of safeguarding services during his time in office, and was frustrated by the lack of response to this from other members.

12.17 From 2009 the Council demonstrated support for the Children and Young People's Service and particularly children's safeguarding by affording the service protection in extremely difficult budgetary circumstances. Budgeted expenditure on Rotherham children's social care increased in real terms by 31.8% in the four years to 2013. This compared with an average increase of 2.6% for its benchmarking group. [20] This increase in expenditure on children's safeguarding is reflected in its relative position in the benchmarking group. In the four years to 2013/4, it went from having the lowest spend (£406 per child) to being at the median of the group (£604 per child).

12.18 Spend on youth services has been severely reduced from £2.4m in 2010/11 to £1.85m in 2012/13.

---

[20] Rotherham's 'statistical neighbours' or benchmarking comparators for children's safeguarding services include Barnsley, Tameside, Wigan, Wakefield, St Helen's, Redcar and Cleveland, Doncaster, Dudley, Telford and Wrekin and Hartlepool.

13. The Role of Elected Members and Senior Officers of the Council

In the early years there seems to have been a prevalent denial of the existence of child sexual exploitation in the Borough, let alone its increasing incidence and dangers. By 2005, it is hard to believe that any senior officers or members from the Leader and the Chief Executive downwards, were not aware of the issue. Most members showed little obvious leadership or interest in CSE for much of the period under review apart from their continued support for Risky Business. The possible reasons for this are not clear but may include denial that this could occur in Rotherham, concern that the ethnic element could damage community cohesion, worry about reputational risk to the Borough if the issue was brought fully into the public domain, and the belief that if that occurred, it might compromise police operations.

For much of the time, senior officers did little to keep members fully informed of the scale and seriousness of the problem, on occasion telling members they believed it was exaggerated. In the early years a small group of frontline professionals from the Council, the Police and Health worked together on CSE, both on individual cases and on issues such as multi-agency procedures. They alerted senior staff to the scale of the abuse but were met with disbelief and left with little management support for the good work they were trying to do. There are reports that senior staff conveyed that sexual exploitation and the ethnicity of perpetrators should be played down. This seemed to be reinforced by the Police. The source of this attitude cannot easily be identified. Concern about the resources CSE could consume; greater priority given to the protection of younger children; professional jealousies, and personal attitudes of some Council staff and the Police towards the girls involved have all been cited as reasons for the failure to address the seriousness and scale of the problem.

The prevailing culture at the most senior level of the Council, until 2009, as described by several people, was bullying and 'macho', and not an appropriate climate in which to discuss the rape and sexual exploitation of young people. From late 2009, the Chief Executive and the Lead Member took a strong personal interest in tackling child sexual exploitation.

13.1 This chapter examines the leadership and management contribution of elected members and senior officers of the Council during the period 1997 - 2013, and how their actions may have impacted on the way in which CSE was handled within the Borough.

The Chief Executives

13.2 From 1997 to date, there were five chief executives of the Council, plus one other who 'acted up' in the role for brief periods. All were interviewed in the course of the Inquiry. Three issues were common to all their statements. These were:

   a) that the overriding priority of the Council for much of that time was economic regeneration and addressing unemployment;

   b) that the Council rarely had enough resources to meet the needs of its population; and

c) that the service priority for improvement in the earlier years was education, and particularly schools.

13.3 The two chief executives in post until 2000 could recall nothing about CSE being an issue during their tenure.

13.4 The Chief Executive (2001-2003) described himself as 'genuinely shocked and surprised' at what had emerged in Rotherham. He had no recollection of it being a major issue. His memory of the Risky Business project was also slight, regarding it as being on the margins of the Council's activity. He did recall that the Home Office research and report were treated as 'anecdotal, using partial information and not methodologically sound' and that the Police were very angry about it.

13.5 His successor (2004-2009) was aware of Risky Business and the presentations that were made to Council members and others. Taking account of the advice he received, he recognised that there was a problem of CSE in Rotherham but he had no reason to believe that the problem was greater than anywhere else. He had a vague recollection about the 'Task and Finish' group, chaired by the Council Leader. He did not recall hearing of Angie Heal 's reports in 2003 and 2006. He was the first chair of the Rotherham Children's Safeguarding Board, for a period of 18 months, but CSE did not feature much in the Board's work at that time. He described tensions amongst the main agencies, mostly between the NHS and children's social care. There were stark differences in thresholds for intervention, in which CSE was not mentioned as a priority. A main focus of his time in office as Chief Executive was to improve external partnership working, which he believed had been achieved by 2009. External partnership had been 'poor' with the Council perceived as overbearing and too dominant. He believed that relations with the Police, and other agencies, had improved markedly during his five years. He could not recall his Director of Education raising concerns with him in 2004 about the police response to problems in secondary schools, as referred to below.

13.6 The present Chief Executive took up post in October 2009. He reported that at the time of his appointment, CSE was not mentioned by members as one of the key challenges he would face. Nor did the previous Chief Executive alert him to the issue. Nor were other major problems such as the Council's budget crisis raised. The Ofsted report that led to the Government putting the Council's children's safeguarding services into 'intervention' in December 2009 did not specifically mention CSE. He knew about it in the context of safeguarding, and Operation Central. He also became aware of the issue at the time of the murder of Child S, when the senior investigating police involved were adamant that it was not linked to CSE, but was an honour killing. That was the message that the Council Leader followed. The next relevant event for him was Operation Chard, in which there were 11 arrests but no prosecutions.

13.7 His own early assessment was that the Council was not self aware or willing to face all of the problems it had. The approach generally was 'not to rock the boat'. When he arrived, he thought that the whole of children's social care seemed to be in denial about its problems. Several people confirmed that the Chief Executive took a direct interest in the change and improvement process required in the Children and Young People's Service from 2010 onwards. Several managers described the Chief Executive, the Lead Member and the Executive Director of Children's Services as having provided excellent support during a difficult period.

Children and Young People's Services

13.8   From 1997 to 2005, there was a Department of Social Services in the Council. Following legislation, children's and adult social services were split, and children's social care was combined with education, to form a Department of Children's Services. There was one Director of Social Services in post from the late 1990s until 2005, and two subsequent Directors of Children's Services, the second of whom is in post at the time of writing. All were interviewed for the Inquiry.

13.9   From 2004 to 2009, there was one Director of Safeguarding. From 2009 to date, there have been four post holders, with a fifth appointed to take up post from August 2014.

13.10 All of the above were interviewed for the Inquiry with the exception of one of the Directors of Safeguarding.

13.11 From the late 1990s, there was an increasing knowledge and awareness of CSE amongst a small number of frontline staff. The multi-agency Key Players Group was set up to maintain an overview of the situation and continued until 2003. It was chaired by the ACPC Child Protection Co-ordinator. They discussed individual cases and also tried to map networks of perpetrators from available intelligence. None of the minutes of meetings of this group have survived, as referred to previously in this report.

13.12 We spoke to some members of the Key Players Group, and gained the impression of dedicated professional people who understood the severity of the problem and were not listened to. They drafted the first set of inter-agency procedures for CSE, which were adopted by the Area Child Protection Committee. They had high hopes that this recognition was going to lead to senior people in their agencies giving the issue more attention and more resources. It did not. 'From then on, it all seemed to go backwards. You were made to feel you were making a fuss about these girls,' said one member. There was general disbelief in the problem they described. Senior managers 'slimmed down' the membership and revised the remit, and another opportunity was lost for the agencies concerned to confront the true scale of the issue and give it the support it needed.

13.13 In 2001-2002, the Director of Education (2001-2005) was one of the first senior officers to raise concerns about CSE with the Police. The heads of three secondary schools had told her of their concerns about young girls being picked up at the school gates by taxi drivers and their suspicions were that this was for the purpose of abuse. Police watched the schools in unmarked cars for a period of time but the problem persisted. She described raising this three times with the Police at a senior level. On the last occasion she described how she was shown a map of the north of England overlaid with various crime networks including 'Drugs', 'Guns', and ' Murder'. She was told that the Police were only interested in putting resources into catching 'the ring leaders' who perpetrated these crimes. She was told that if they were caught, her local problems would cease. She found this an unacceptable response, which ignored the abuse of children. Her Chair at the time also raised the issue with the Police, according to this officer. The District Commander (2001-2005) could not recall these conversations but was aware of the police action with secondary schools.

13.14 From an early stage, children's social care managers seemed reluctant to accept the extent of the problem of CSE within the Borough. There were constant difficulties over the allocation of referrals from Risky Business. In 2004, the Sexual Exploitation Forum minutes indicated concerns raised by Risky Business that some referrals they were making to children's social care were being reclassified e.g.'Teenager out of control'. A further minuted example was that of a project worker attempting to make a referral and being told that she had to have witnessed the incident herself as third party information would not be accepted. The long-standing tensions between the Risky Business project and children's social care are described in Chapter 9. As already stated, the clear responsibility for resolving these tensions lay with those in charge of children's social care and youth services, who failed to do so over many years.

13.15 From 2003 onwards, Directors of Safeguarding were regularly reporting problems with recruitment and retention of social workers in a series of reports to their Lead Member.

13.16 They described the negative impact this was having on services. These acute staffing problems persisted in one form or another until 2010. A 2003 Social Services Inspectorate report found that core services were under pressure and this was 'not fully appreciated by the Council'. This was compounded by staff vacancies. Children's social care received one star gradings in 2003 and 2004.

13.17 In 2004, a report was taken to the Cabinet Member for Social Services advising that vacancy levels meant that it was not possible to allocate a number of cases, and that the budget would be overspent. It was recommended that monthly rather than quarterly reports be submitted in order to monitor concerns.

13.18 In December 2005, a joint paper from Police and Children and Young People's Services was taken to the Safeguarding Board proposing significant changes to the Rotherham service delivery response to CSE. It was recommended that Risky Business become a multi agency resource by September 2006, and that the Sexual Exploitation Forum become more strategic, limiting the discussion of individual cases. It was also agreed that the Forum would produce an Annual Report each January.

13.19 The Police carried out an audit of 87 files in 2005, which resulted in them proposing that large numbers of girls be removed from the Sexual Exploitation Forum monitoring process. Risky Business challenged the factual accuracy and completeness of some of the information in the audit, raising serious concerns about many of the girls involved, where it was recommended they be removed from monitoring. The Police reason for removing several girls from monitoring was they were pregnant or had given birth. All looked after children were removed from the list. Several of the cases removed from monitoring were read by the Inquiry and we found Risky Business concerns to be valid. It is hard to avoid the conclusion that the Police, supported by children's social care, were intent on reducing the number of names on Forum monitoring for CSE.

13.20 The minutes of the Sexual Exploitation Forum in 2005 and 2006 showed continuing tensions between Risky Business and children's social care over the removal of girls from Forum monitoring if they became child protection cases or were followed up by children's social care. There were also concerns recorded about Strategy meetings not being convened when Risky Business requested them. A report to the Safeguarding Board in June 2007 stated that there were no children on the Child Protection Register due to issues of sexual exploitation and only two children looked after by the local authority had been identified as at risk of sexual exploitation. Given the large number of referrals for CSE known about within the statutory agencies at that time, and the seriousness of the circumstances of individual children, confirmed by the Inquiry's file reading, these figures suggest that the council was failing to use its statutory powers to protect these children. There is no record in the minutes of any challenge to these figures.

13.21 By 2008-09, more committed and focused leadership of CSE was apparent in the CYPS. The appointment in 2007 of a part time lead for CSE contributed to this. The person appointed was seen by all of those involved as a positive influence on the difficulties between Risky Business and the children's social care staff, especially in getting individual cases allocated. She was described by one interviewee as providing 'a straight pathway to social work'.

13.22 She told the Inquiry that it was certainly conveyed by senior managers in the CYP service that the extent of CSE was being exaggerated. A divide amongst senior managers was also obvious. CSE was not seen as a priority at that time, especially by some operational locality managers, who also thought Risky Business were exaggerating, and had a high volume of competing priorities to meet. Her unequivocal view was that the project accurately reflected the scale and seriousness of the problem, even if their presentation was sometimes unorthodox.

13.23 From 2005 onwards, the post of Director of Safeguarding was the strategic and operational head of the children and families service, reporting to the Executive Director of Children's Services, who should be assumed to have owned overarching responsibility for the service response to CSE. However, in the structure of children's services at that time, others at the same level had their own interests and responsibilities that overlapped with safeguarding, such as the directors for performance management and youth services. There were seven directors in total. 'A lot of in-fighting' amongst them was reported to the Inquiry. In the present structure, there are two directors reporting to the Executive Director of Children's Services.

13.24 The Children Act (2004) required all local authorities to establish integrated children's services by April 2008. The Director of Children's Services (2005 – 2008) continued the development programme initiated by her predecessor. This was a local interpretation of the vision contained in the Government guidance 'Every Child Matters'. The focus was on the delivery of co-located services and management within localities. Seven localities were created, each with two managers who supervised children's social care. It appeared that frontline staff whose jobs were affected were not ready for the culture change that the reorganisation required. This reorganisation was reported to consume a large amount of staff time and energy. It was seen by some, both internally and in outside agencies, as diverting staff from their core function of delivering quality services. It began in 2005 and was not concluded by the time the Director of Children's Services left in 2008. At that point, integration of frontline services was still in progress. Some of the managers appointed were not professionally qualified social workers and some who were lacked child protection experience.

13.25 The Annual Performance Assessment letter for Children and Young People's Services in 2005 stated that staff turnover and sickness absence in social services were too high. This was addressed by various recruitment initiatives. By 2007, turnover of social workers had improved and vacancy levels had dropped to 14%, but this was not sustained. In mid-2008, the vacancy rate was reported as over 40% at its worst, and in 2009 was 37%.

13.26 The Ofsted Joint Area Review report in 2006 was very positive. However, it contained the astonishing statement that 'it appeared that vulnerable children and young people are kept safe from abuse and exploitation'. This was not qualified in any way. From the evidence described in Chapter 5 of this report, this was not an accurate reflection of the situation, and may have served to give false reassurance to those running the service.

13.27 Ofsted's evaluation of children's social care, which had been previously rated as Good, started to decline. In the period April 2007 – March 2008, covered by the 2008 Annual Performance Assessment, it was judged overall as Adequate. Specifically, Management of Children and Young People's Services was judged Adequate. Important weaknesses included that management oversight of looked after children had not ensured they had been fully safeguarded.

13.28 Set against a background of rising demand, high vacancies amongst social workers and their managers, and reliance on agency staff to cover frontline posts, the persistence with the reorganisation at that time might be seen as ill judged. Several managers described the situation around 2007 onwards as 'chaotic'. Other frontline staff expressed the same view; the service appeared to have lacked the capacity to implement a radical and highly complex reorganisation; and there was co-location but no agreed line management arrangements. Waiting for the formal transfer of staff to be agreed created organisational 'inertia', according to some. In the end the process was not completed.

13.29 The current Executive Director of Children's Services had supported the integration model of her predecessor but in 2009 determined it was not working and that 'the basics' were not right. The Council and NHS Rotherham commissioned Children First to carry out an external review of children's services. Reporting in May 2009, one of the overall findings of the review was that 'Recent restructures have served to create a complex and excessive number of teams and panels, which can lead to confusion and increase risk. These require urgent rationalisation so that management lines and performance accountabilities are absolutely clear and understood. The number of panels relating to vulnerable children must be reviewed and rationalised to ensure clarity, simplicity and manageable structures for all staff.'

13.30 The 2009 report also looked at Rotherham's resourcing of children's services, in comparison to its benchmarking group. It found that the Council had very high levels of expenditure on schools and nursery schools, but in contrast spending on most children's social care services was relatively low, with spend on looked after children especially low. The report questioned whether the resourcing of some high-risk services was sufficient.

13.31 The first police operation in Rotherham to address multiple perpetrators of CSE was Operation Central, in 2008. This was commended by many as an excellent example of joint working between the Council and the Police.

13.32 Following the success of Operation Central, in 2009 the Police initiated Operation Czar. On this occasion, children's social care would take a leading role and Risky Business was told to close all its cases of young people who were to be included in this Operation as children's social care would allocate them to social workers. Apart from the questionable practice of fracturing the relationships of these girls with Risky Business staff, the evidence from file reading showed that some of those victims were amongst the most serious cases of child sexual exploitation.

13.33 Operation Czar was not a success. It is not clear who precisely amongst the senior officers took the decision to involve children's social care as the lead, without proper preparation at the frontline, but it proved unwise in the event. The Executive Director of Children's Services (2008 to date) described how they 'tried to use the same methodology and approach as Central, but it didn't work'. She was asked to secure funding for two extra social workers for the operation, which she did.

13.34 Children's social care staff had no previous experience of this activity. The girls did not trust them. They removed some of these girls from home and then returned them within days, and many became closed cases very quickly after the Operation was over, leaving them with no support. One young social worker involved described the authority as 'a scary place to be in 2009'. She was 21, newly qualified and had never had a practice placement in a local authority. About Operation Czar, she said 'nobody knew what they were supposed to be doing. Just firefighting. We attended loads of meetings. We were always ten paces behind the perpetrators. Everyone involved wanted to do a good job on Czar but it was all badly managed.' Some Abduction Notices were served, but there were no arrests.

13.35 By late 2009, when the Minister of State served an Improvement Notice on the Council for its children's safeguarding services, there is no doubt that the systems and operations for protecting Rotherham's children were unsafe. The Director of Safeguarding (2010-11) described what she found on taking up post. There were significant vacancies; a lot of agency staff were being used; there was a lack of management oversight; poor accountability for casework; poor monitoring of unallocated work; poor monitoring of assessment times; looked after children lacked plans in some instances; quality of practice was generally weak and the complexity of cases was very high; the quality of professional supervision was poor, sometimes provided by managers who were not social work qualified. Staff were overwhelmed, and disempowered, and felt senior staff were 'invisible'. Despite this context, she saw no complacency about CSE. The Inquiry concluded that the quality and extent of children's social care support to the young people who were victims or at risk must surely have suffered.

13.36 There ensued a great deal of work to reform systems and put in place quality assurance and performance management processes. The structure of the service was revised; professional supervision of social workers was provided only by social work managers who were experienced in child protection. Social workers who were in post in 2009 described the experience now to be 'unrecognisable' because of these improvements.

13.37 Following the publication of the Home Affairs Select Committee report in June 2013, a report to the Cabinet by the Executive Director of Children's Services stated that 'Tackling the sexual exploitation of children and young people remains the highest priority for Rotherham Borough Council'. It also recommended that a quarterly report on progress against the local child sexual exploitation Action Plan be brought to Cabinet.

Role, Remit and Location of the CSE team

13.38 A Safeguarding Coordinator for CSE was appointed in 2010. She had an unhelpful beginning in her role, with seven changes of manager in her first year in post. She subsequently took over responsibility for the children's social care staff in the newly established CSE team.

13.39 We met the staff group and managers in the joint CSE team and were impressed by their motivation and obvious commitment to the children they were working to protect. Several people in children's social care told us that the role and remit of the team needed to be clarified as a matter of urgency, and this was long overdue. There were no protocols setting out how the team should interface with other parts of the children's social care. The Service Manager responsible for the team did not know whether the team had a written remit.

13.40 At the time of the Inquiry, the team was short staffed because of staff illness. The Service Manager responsible for the team considered that adequate cover arrangements had been made but this was not a view shared by those directly responsible for managing team members. The team has three qualified social workers but deals with a significant number of complex cases as well as offering preventive services, and co-working cases with other teams. Several experienced managers told us that the current arrangements are not sustainable and action needed to be taken to resolve this.

13.41 By contrast, the police officers responsible for CSE in Rotherham considered that the police input to the CSE team was extremely clear and well understood. The police function in the team is well resourced (6 detectives) and has a clear focus. We learned that joint work is sometimes delayed because children's social care is under-resourced compared to the police capacity. From the evidence, we were satisfied that at the time of the Inquiry, CSE was well resourced by the Police and suitably responsive to need.

13.42 There was considerable support from the Police for strengthening the social care resources in the team and moving from a co-located to a jointly managed team. The Police also viewed the establishment of the Multi-agency Safeguarding Hub (MASH), scheduled to take place in August 2014, as a major opportunity to improve and strengthen safeguarding work in Rotherham and all agencies should make this a priority.

13.43 We received some comments that it was impossible for a small team to deal with all CSE issues, and important that the whole of children's social care had the capacity to safeguard exploited children. This was raised as an issue in the recent diagnostic report completed by the Safeguarding Board Chair. We share the concerns many expressed that in the absence of a central team, the focus on child exploitation would become diluted.

The Role of Elected Members

13.44 In 2004-2005, a series of presentations on CSE were first made to councillors and then other relevant groups and agencies, led by the external manager of Risky Business, from Youth Services. The presentations were unambiguous about the nature and extent of the problem. They included the following information:

a) a description of CSE in Rotherham and its impact on children as young as 12;

b) the scale of the problem;

c) the exercise of control through drugs, rape and physical force. In Rotherham, 55% of such children had used heroin at least once per week; 40% had been raped; 73% had sexual health problems; 33% had attempted suicide. Most had self harmed; and

d) the section on perpetrators mentioned an Asian family involved with taxi firms, and identified 50 people, 45 of whom were Asian, 4 were white, and 1 African-Caribbean.

13.45 Attendees were provided with background information listing the known addresses of alleged activity, including hotels and takeaways in Rotherham. It also included taxi companies alleged to be involved, and case studies of three girls. In total, Risky Business supported 319 girls on either a one to one or group work basis over an 18-month period from April 2004 until October 2005. The presentation was made at the end of 2004 to the Rotherham Children and Young People's Board, with six councillors present, including the Leader. The following April, a further presentation was made to 30 councillors. The explicit content meant that by 2005 few members or senior officers could say 'we didn't know'. Similar material had been passed to the Police in 2001 by Risky Business on behalf of the local agencies.

13.46 In response to these growing concerns about sexual exploitation in Rotherham, a Task and Finish group was set up in December 2004, chaired by the Leader of the Council. Only one minute of its meetings (March 2005) was available, though other minutes contained references to this group's work. The March minute listed a number of actions including multi agency training, a local publicity campaign and appointing a Co-ordinator on the issue, though this did not seem to happen until 2007. In November 2005, the Chair of the Children and Young People's Voluntary Sector Consortium wrote to the Chief Executive, expressing concern at the problem of child sexual exploitation in Rotherham and recalling that members of the Consortium gave evidence to the Task and Finish Group on March 2. The Consortium had not been represented at any meetings after that. She requested a progress report on the Group's work. The Chief Executive's reply has not been found. In late 2005, the Group agreed that more awareness training around CSE needed to be provided within the child protection training programme. There is no further record of this group's meetings or its outputs or how it ceased to exist.

13.47 At several points from the early 2000s onwards, members increased the funding to

Risky Business, in recognition of its valuable work. Members also responded to the funding pressures experienced by children's social care over many years by affording protection to the service when significant savings were required, in particular from 2008 onwards. Nevertheless, it should be noted that Rotherham started at a low base of funding for children's social care, compared to its neighbours, and whatever protection afforded did not fully compensate for the underlying lack of investment and rising demand.

13.48 The Lead Member for CYP (2005 - 2010), who later became the South Yorkshire Police and Crime Commissioner, was aware of CSE from the outset of his tenure, and believed that reports on the subject which he regularly received as Lead Member were taken seriously and acted upon by the Council in conjunction with the Police. This was stated in his written evidence to the Home Affairs Select Committee in 2013, where he also stated that race was never presented to him by staff or agencies as an obstacle to investigating offences.

13.49 In 2006, a Conservative councillor requested a meeting with the Council Leader at which he expressed his concerns about CSE. This had come to his attention via constituents. He told the Inquiry that the Council Leader advised him the matters were being dealt with by the Police and requested that he did not raise them publicly.

13.50 Latterly, in 2012/13 further CSE training sessions for councillors were organised with the attendance being 60 out of 63 councillors.

13.51 Interviews with senior members revealed that none could recall the issue ever being discussed in the Labour Group until 2012. Given the seriousness of the subject, the evidence available, and the reputational damage to the Council, it is extraordinary that the Labour Group, which dominated the Council, failed to discuss CSE until then. Some senior members acknowledged that that was a mistake. Asked if they should have done things differently, they thought that as an administration they should have tackled the issues 'head on', including any concerns about ethnic issues.

13.52 The terms used by many people we spoke to about how those in authority (members and some officers) dealt with CSE were 'sweeping it under the carpet', 'turning a blind eye' and 'keeping a lid on it'. One person said of the past 'the people above just didn't want to know'.

13.53 In September 2013, the Council Leader apologised 'unreservedly' to those young people who had been let down by the safeguarding services, which prior to 2009 'simply weren't good enough'. He reiterated that the safeguarding of young people was the Council 's highest priority and announced that an independent inquiry would be held.

The Scrutiny Function

13.54 Overview and scrutiny committees may make recommendations to the Council's

Executive. Under other legislation the Council's scrutiny committee may also make recommendations to other local bodies. Many scrutiny functions have a process by which recommendations are monitored to check on their implementation. This is seen as one of the principal ways in which to ascertain the impact that scrutiny has on local services. In 2005, the Children's and Young People's Scrutiny Panel was set up. This included up to 12 elected members. In 2006, the Looked After Children Scrutiny Sub-Panel was set up, with 11 elected members. It was disbanded in 2010 and replaced by the Corporate Parenting Group, with six elected members. There was also an Overview and Scrutiny Management Board, which reviewed what all the separate scrutiny panels were discussing. Since 2012, there are four Select Commissions for scrutiny, replacing the previous panels. Each non-executive councillor is entitled to be a member of at least one of four of the Select Commissions.

13.55 The Chair of the Children and Young People's Select Commission has been in that role for the past eleven years. She attended the members' seminar on CSE in 2005 and knew about the Leader's Task and Finish Group. She was confident that she had challenged officials, but over the years she had faced obstacles to her work as Chair. When the majority of members belonged to one party, it was not easy for a Commission to maintain its total independence. In her experience, agenda items were too often presented as faits accomplis, already wrapped and sealed. She recalled raising the issue of CSE in 2008 with the Lead Member and the Director of Children's Services, specifically about why certain things had not been done. She described how she was given assurance that all was in hand and that she would be informed on a 'need to know' basis. Again, in 2009, she reported that she asked for information about CSE and received the same message. She was confident, however, that the recent appointment of new senior members would lead to more open and effective scrutiny within the Council.

13.56 A meeting of the Overview and Scrutiny Management Board took place in October 2012, and was largely devoted to the Child S Serious Case Review. The minute reflects one example of rigorous challenge of the issues raised by the review.

Accountability

13.57 The Inquiry Team has read the minutes and proceedings of the various member groups that have an interest in child sexual exploitation, including meetings of the Council, the Cabinet and the Lead Member for Children and Young People's Services. While acknowledging that reading minutes is not the same as witnessing the meetings themselves, we gained two broad impressions. The first is that the same item seemed to have to go through an inordinate number of council meetings and other bodies before gaining acceptance. Admittedly, there is a 'need to know' in many instances, but more important is the possibility that this arrangement blunts accountability. An issue or responsibility that belongs to everybody effectively belongs to nobody, and in the case of sexual exploitation of children in Rotherham, accountability was key.

13.58 Even more significant is the apparent lack of effective scrutiny exercised by these several groups or bodies, and least of all by the Scrutiny Panels. Scrutiny in its widest sense is an essential component of Cabinet government. Rarely does it appear from the minutes that councillors have held officers to account by checking the evidence for proposals or asking whether their ends could be met in other ways. It may be that the minutes are written in bland, non-specific, language, but that does nothing to reassure the public that genuine accountability is being exercised. It is important that councillors test proposals by reference to their broad experience and their knowledge of the Borough and their own constituents. There should be nothing threatening about this; good officers should welcome challenge as a central part of local democracy.

13.59 The Inquiry team found several instances where important issues were not reported to members. As has been described, senior officers of the Council were made aware of the increasing seriousness of CSE from an early stage, and members' seminars were arranged in 2004-05. Yet in July of 2005, the sexual exploitation of young people failed to feature in a report to the Cabinet Member for CYPS entitled 'State of the Nation', intended to summarise the main issues for children's services in the Borough, along with strengths, weaknesses and risks.

13.60 Some people we interviewed suspected that a small number of those with political authority in the Council had links to the perpetrators of CSE through taxi firms and other business or family interests. We were told by the Police that there was no evidence to support these suspicions.

Organisational Culture

13.61 Organisational culture is a powerful force that guides decisions and actions. It has a potent effect on the organisation's well-being and effectiveness. The Council has a duty to provide effective corporate services. In relation to CSE, the long-term benefit of children will only be served by Council departments working together in a spirit of shared commitment and mutual confidence.

13.62 Executive 'leaders' play a large part in defining organisational culture by what they say and what they do. In this respect, leaders such as senior officers and members in a Council should model good behaviour for their staff groups and others in setting the tone for their shared endeavour to deliver the best possible services. This includes values, attitudes and working language.

13.63 As far back as 1998, the then Chief Executive was able to say that senior women officers in the Council were not readily accepted either by officers or members. The Chief Executive from 2004 to 2009 had no sense of a particularly 'macho' culture but was aware that a small number of senior councillors could be aggressive and intimidating to officers.

13.64 The Leader of the Council, from 2000 to 2003, agreed that the culture overall was 'macho' and sexist. He referred specifically to three members accessing adult pornography on council computers, which he had to deal with. He also referred to the bullying behaviour of some members towards the then Chief Executive, probably because he and the Chief Executive were attempting to improve and modernise a council which was underperforming, which had a very traditional culture, which was 'slow to change' and which had come to the attention of inspectors and government (albeit mainly for school buildings rather than children's safeguarding). One of the current Cabinet members who had been in the Council since 1999 also agreed with the description of bullying and strong male dominance. The Deputy Leader (2011 – 2014) also agreed. Of the group of people interviewed, many confirmed this perception.

13.65 A succession of senior officers, past and present, male and female, who were interviewed for the Inquiry raised the negative culture as being an issue from 1997 to 2009. Their remarks and some of the less offensive quotations from a small number of senior officers and members are given below:

> 'The member barometer re sexual matters was skewed'
>
> 'It was a very grubby environment in which to work'
>
> 'A colleague was told she ought to wear shorter skirts to meetings and she'd get on better'
>
> 'A senior member said on four occasions in public places "you women are only fit for cooking, washing and darning" '
>
> 'A senior member said I know what I'd like to do to you if I was ten years' younger'
>
> 'A senior member asked me if I wore a mask while having sex'

13.66 One of the senior managers in Safeguarding stated that she wrote to a previous Chief Executive more than once about the conduct of members, but the Inquiry was unable to obtain copies of these letters from the Council.

13.67 A senior officer was described by several people as being bullied and badly treated until the arrival of the present Chief Executive who took action on this behaviour.

13.68 In October 2009, the outgoing Director of Safeguarding wrote to the Chief Executive referring to a recent budget meeting chaired by the Lead Member for Children and Young People's Services. The following account is taken from her letter. A senior officer present, not from Safeguarding Services, was quoted as saying that in his professional view Rotherham had too many looked after children and this accounted for a significant part of the overspend. When challenged for his evidence for this assertion he is described as becoming aggressive and antagonistic. He was asked to stop shouting. He responded by saying that shouting was the only way to get through to these people and he persisted for over an hour, swearing frequently, with no intervention from the Chair, according to the letter. The Director of Safeguarding described the experience as being 'intimidating, humiliating, bullying and entirely professionally unacceptable.' She concluded by saying she only felt able to put this in writing because she was leaving the authority.

13.69 The existence of such a culture as described above is likely to have impeded the Council from providing an effective, corporate response to such a highly sensitive social problem as child sexual exploitation.

14. Recommendations

14.1 As a consequence of several reviews, reports and inspections over the last two years, the Council, its partners and the Safeguarding Board are already in receipt of many recommendations for improvement in their approach to CSE. The Safeguarding Board has brought these together into a single document. It includes the recommendations from the CSE Diagnostic Report, the Barnardo's CSE Practice Review, the HMIC South Yorkshire Police Response to CSE, and the report of the Office of the Children's Commissioner. The document is reproduced in Appendix 5.

14.2 The Inquiry took the view that it was unnecessary to repeat the recommendations listed in these reports. We have identified 15 areas which we consider should be a priority.

14.3 It should also be noted that the National Working Group Network on Tackling Child Sexual Exploitation has also recently produced a 'Summary of Recommendations for All Agencies', from a range of reports, inquiries, serious case reviews and research. This provides a helpful checklist, which could be used by the Council and its partners in conjunction with the list compiled by the Safeguarding Board.

Risk assessment

Recommendation 1: Senior managers should ensure that there are up-to-date risk assessments on all children affected by CSE. These should be of consistently high quality and clearly recorded on the child's file.

Recommendation 2: The numeric scoring tool should be kept under review. Professional judgements about risk should be clearly recorded where these are not adequately captured by the numeric tool.

Looked after children

Recommendation 3: Managers should develop a more strategic approach to protecting looked after children who are sexually exploited. This must include the use of out-of-area placements. The Borough should work with other authorities to minimise the risks of sexual exploitation to all children, including those living in placements where they may become exposed to CSE. The strategy should include improved arrangements for supporting children in out-of-area placements when they require leaving care services.

Outreach and accessibility

Recommendation 4: The Council should make every effort to make help reach out to victims of CSE who are not yet in touch with services. In particular, it should make every effort to restore open access and outreach work with children affected by CSE to the level previously provided by Risky Business.

Joint CSE team

Recommendation 5: The remit and responsibilities of the joint CSE team should be urgently decided and communicated to all concerned in a way that leaves no room for doubt.

Recommendation 6: Agencies should commit to introducing a single manager for the multi-agency CSE team. This should be implemented as quickly as possible.

Recommendation 7: The Council, together with the Police, should review the social care resources available to the CSE team, and make sure these are consistent with the need and demand for services.

Collaboration within CYPS

Recommendation 8: Wider children's social care, the CSE team and integrated youth and support services should work better together to ensure that children affected by CSE are well supported and offered an appropriate range of preventive services.

Ongoing work with victims

Recommendation 9: All services should recognise that once a child is affected by CSE, he or she is likely to require support and therapeutic intervention for an extended period of time. Children should not be offered short-term intervention only, and cases should not be closed prematurely.

Post abuse support

Recommendation 10: The Safeguarding Board, through the CSE Sub-group, should work with local agencies, including health, to secure the delivery of post-abuse support services.

Quality Assurance

Recommendation 11: All agencies should continue to resource, and strengthen, the quality assurance work currently underway under the auspices of the Safeguarding Board.

Minority ethnic communities

Recommendation 12: There should be more direct and more frequent engagement by the Council and also the Safeguarding Board with women and men from minority ethnic communities on the issue of CSE and other forms of abuse.

Recommendation 13: The Safeguarding Board should address the under-reporting of sexual exploitation and abuse in minority ethnic communities.

The issue of race

Recommendation 14: The issue of race should be tackled as an absolute priority if it is a significant factor in the criminal activity of organised child sexual abuse in the Borough.

Serious Case Reviews

Recommendation 15: We recommend to the Department of Education that the guiding principle on redactions in Serious Case Reviews must be that the welfare of any children involved is paramount.

Appendix 1: Terms of Reference for the Independent Inquiry into Child Sexual Exploitation 1997 - 2013

Basis

1. That it be conducted by an independent person with appropriate skills, experience and abilities who has not previously been employed by or undertaken work, either directly or indirectly, for Rotherham Metropolitan Borough Council, nor is a relation of any member or officer of the Council past or present. Prior to appointment the independent person will be required to sign a declaration to that effect. The person should be on a list of reputable persons recommended to the Council by the Local Government Association.

2. That the author is able to commission such specialist support that they may need to fulfil the terms of reference specifically relating to social care practice regarding child sexual exploitation and that any such person engaged also be required to meet the terms set out in 1 above and sign a declaration to that effect. Commissioning of such support shall be in consultation with the Chief Executive and within the budgetary limits agreed.

3. That the author be supported by the Council's Monitoring Officer, who will provide relevant legal advice and commission specialist advice if considered necessary, and by the Council's Director of Human Resources in relation to arranging such interviews with members and officers that the independent person requires.

4. That the Inquiry's status is non-statutory. The consequence therefore is that witnesses who no longer work for the Council may only be interviewed with their consent. Current serving officers and members will be required to give evidence to and support the inquiry.

5. That the Inquiry is undertaken in a way that is responsive to the wishes and needs of young people that may have been subject to sexual exploitation in the past.

Scope

6. The inquiry has two distinct elements.

1997 to December 2009

7. Through a process of reviewing an appropriate selection of child sexual exploitation case files from the period the Inquiry will:

   a) Analyse social care practice, information gathering, data recording, data-sharing (specifically between the Council and South Yorkshire Police) and decision making.

b) Consider the application of child sexual exploitation policies, procedures and best practice as they existed at the time.

c) Consider managerial and political oversight, leadership and direction, operational management practice including supervision, support and guidance and the roles and responsibilities of other parties including the Police, Crown Prosecution Service, health services, schools, parents, family and the Local Safeguarding Children Board.

d) Consider emerging evidence, intelligence or trends, how they were communicated within the Council and with other agencies and the speed and way in which Council service delivery was adjusted to respond.

e) Identify who in the Council knew what information when and determine whether that information was used effectively and in the best interests of protecting young people.

f) Examine the extent to which other forms of regulatory control available to the Council and others (for example activities such as licensing and environmental health) were used to inform the safeguarding of children from sexual exploitation.

g) Ensure that the cases reviewed will include those identified in the national press.

8.   The objectives of this element of the review are:

a) To consider whether the Council when exercising its statutory and non-statutory powers could have done more to protect young people from child sexual exploitation and whether the range of options available was in any way limited by the actions of other agencies.

b) To consider whether young people were adequately protected from the risks of sexual exploitation and if not to identify the factors that led to the failure to adequately protect them, including the part played by other agencies.

c) To consider specifically whether there is any evidence of the Council, or any other agency, not taking appropriate action as a consequence of concerns regarding racial or ethnic sensitivities.

d) Make recommendations that can be used by the Council and others to ensure that any of the mistakes of the past are not repeated

December 2009 to January 2013

9.   Through a process of both reviewing an appropriate selection of child sexual exploitation case files and considering evidence placed within the public domain regarding safeguarding services within Rotherham (including Ofsted Inspections and Serious Case Reviews) throughout the period the Inquiry will:

a) Examine whether there is recent and current evidence that recommendations regarding the lessons learned and which have been identified in the first part of the review have been or are in the process of being implemented by the Council.

b) Consider whether there is recent and current evidence the Council has or is in the process of implementing Government policy relating to child sexual exploitation that has been issued within the period.

10. The objectives of this element of the review are:-

   a) To consider whether the Council when exercising its statutory and non - statutory powers could have done more to protect young people from child sexual exploitation and whether the range of options available was in any way limited by the actions of other agencies.

   b) To consider whether there is evidence of necessary improvements to the Council's services and the extent to which the improvements are becoming embedded.

   c) To consider whether there is evidence that the pace of any such improvement is appropriate to the extremely serious nature of previous historic failings to the Council's safeguarding services in general, and child sexual exploitation practices in particular.

   d) To consider specifically whether there is any evidence of the Council, or any other agency not taking appropriate actions as a consequence of concerns regarding racial or ethnic sensitivities.

   e) To make recommendations that can be used by the Council and others.

Performance Management and Governance

11. The terms of reference will be discussed with the author, prior to the Inquiry being undertaken. Any suggested additions or amendments will be considered by and made at the discretion of the Chief Executive and subsequently reported to Cabinet.

12. A draft report and final report will be available by dates to be agreed in writing at the date the Inquiry is commissioned

13. The Inquiry report will be the bona fide opinion of the author and will be endorsed as such.

14. The Inquiry report shall be provided in a format that can be made publicly available. The author shall ensure that the Council's requirement to maximise transparency is met. It is acknowledged that sensitive or confidential information may be referred to in the report and the author should use an appropriate referencing system to ensure the anonymity of clients and that all legal requirements regarding confidentiality and data protection are met.

15. Throughout the duration of the conduct of the inquiry the author shall report on progress to the Chief Executive at the end of each week, in a manner to be agreed in writing.

16.   The identification of cases for review and of officers, members and other contributors for interview shall be entirely at the discretion of the author. However the Council requires that the number and breadth of files reviewed will be sufficiently representative to provide a robust basis for the analysis. Any arrangements for files, record keeping, minutes, interviews to be arranged on request by the Monitoring Officer and/or the Director of Human Resources.

17.   The author shall consider, and consult with the Chief Executive upon, the appropriateness of seeking evidence from the victims of child sexual exploitation.

18.   The final report will be delivered to the Chief Executive, who will report it to Cabinet together with the Council's response. Both reports will be made public.

Appendix 2: Methodology

Reading the files

1. We read a total of 66 case files as part of the fieldwork for the Inquiry. These were selected as follows:

   a) A randomised sample of the CSE caseload as at 30 September 2013 (19 out of 51 cases – a 37% sample)

   b) Three other current cases brought to the attention of the Inquiry team during the course of the fieldwork.

   c) 22 historic cases of victims sampled from police operations, including Central, Czar and Chard.

   d) The case files of three children who were the subject of national media attention.

   e) A randomised sample of 19 other historic cases, taken from a list of 937 names of children associated with CSE. The names were provided to the Inquiry by children's social care, or the Police.

2. In the majority of cases, we read both the Risky Business and the children's social care files. We also had access to residential case files and records kept by foster carers for many of the looked after children. In a small number of cases, the children's social care file could not be traced.

3. Five cases from the total sampled by the Inquiry were reviewed by the National Working Group Network's specialist team. There was a high level of consistency in the judgements made by the Inquiry Team's file reader and the team from the National Working Group Network.

4. The Inquiry had access to the minutes about individual children discussed at the Sexual Exploitation Forum between 2004 and 2006. We also read large numbers of minutes of Strategy meetings about individuals and groups of children, as well as suspected perpetrators, from the early 2000s onwards. The numbers of children discussed in all these minutes ran to many hundreds of children who were being exploited, as well as others who were at serious risk.

5. Minutes of discussions about individuals and groups of children by the Key Players meeting (late 90s to around 2004) could not be traced for the purposes of the Inquiry, and could not be scrutinised.

6. In the course of reading files, we had sight of internal correspondence identifying children who had been sexually exploited, and the concerns their parents had expressed. We read correspondence in the files where parents had detailed their children's experiences and their concerns about inadequate responses by the statutory agencies. We were also contacted by several parents via the confidential email and Freepost addresses.

Document analysis

7.   The Inquiry team studied a very large number of Rotherham Council Committee minutes, and papers and minutes of the Safeguarding Board and its predecessor, the Area Child Protection Committee.

8.   We also read relevant national and local reports produced by external agencies. Details are given in Chapters 2 and 3, and in Appendices 4 and 5.

Fieldwork interviews

9.   We interviewed a large number of people from local agencies. We give a list of these in Appendix 3[21]. In summary, the Inquiry covered:

Meeting /Interview	No
Individual interviews with current staff of Rotherham Borough Council	27
Staff met in a group meeting with the joint CSE team	9
Staff met in group meetings (team managers, independent reviewing officers & conference chairs, social workers, residential managers and personal advisors with the Bridges project)	17
Individual interviews with former staff of the Borough	18
Current elected members	6
Former elected members	5
Serving police officers	7
Former police officers	4
Young people met (Care Leavers' Group, Youth Cabinet representatives and Focus group of young people and others)	24
Specialists from the National Working Group Network (4 meetings)	4
People from other agencies, voluntary organisations and community groups	14

---

[21] The Council provided the Inquiry with the dates when people were employed in Rotherham.

Appendix 3: List of interviewees

Rotherham Metropolitan Borough Council

Staff

Martin Kimber	Chief Executive
Joyce Thacker	Executive Director, Children and Young People's Services
Jacqueline Collins	Director of Legal Services
Warren Carratt	Service Manager (Strategy, Standards and Early Help)
Catherine Eshelby	Principal Practitioner
Chris Brodhurst-Brown	Head of Integrated Youth Support Services
Zafar Saleem	Community Engagement Manager
Waheed Akhtar	Community Engagement Officer
Clair Pyper	Interim Director of Safeguarding Children and Families
Claire Edgar	Team Manager, Sexual Exploitation Team
Lynne Grice-Saddington	Manager, Rights-to-Rights Service
Joanne Robertson	Finance Manager
Pete Hudson	Chief Finance Manager
David Richmond	Director of Housing and Neighbourhood Services
Alan Pogorzelec	Business Regulation Manager
Linda Alcock	Safeguarding Unit Manager
Phil Morris	Business Manager, Safeguarding Board
Kevin Stevens	Safeguarding Quality Assurance Officer
Chris Seekings	Quality Assurance Officer
Louise Pashley	Practice Manager, Bridges Project
Kelly White	Service Manager
Kerry Byrne	Partnership and Youth Development Manager
Lorraine Lichfield	Strategic Lead – Education OTAS & Exclusions
Jo Smith	Head of the Rowan Centre
John Radford	Director of Public Health
Joanna Saunders	Head of Health Improvement
Anna Clack	Public Health Specialist

Group Meetings of staff

Independent Reviewing Officers and Conference Chairs
Social Workers
Residential Managers
Team Managers
Child Sexual Exploitation Team
Bridges Project Personal Advisors

Former staff

Erica Leach	Child Protection Co-ordinator (1998-2003) (worked for the Council 1986-2010)
John Gomersall	Director of Social Services (1999-2006) (worked for the Council 1973-2006)
Ged Fitzgerald	Chief Executive (2001-2003)
Mike Cuff	Chief Executive (2004-2009)
John Bell	Chief Executive (1986-1998)
Alan Carruthers	Chief Executive (1999-2000)
Sonia Sharp	Director of Children's Services (2005-2008)

Di Billups	Executive Director of Education (2001-2005)
Lynn Burns	Interim Director of Safeguarding (2009-2010)
Pam Allen	Director of Safeguarding (2004-2009)
	(worked for the Council 1996-2009)
Jackie Wilson	Head of Function (2002-2007)
	(worked for the Council 1996-2007)
Gani Martins	Director of Safeguarding (2010-2011)
Simon Perry	Director of Targeted Services (2008-2011)
	(worked for the Council 2001-2011)
Viv Woodhead	Assistant Safeguarding Manager (2007-2012)

& Former staff of the Risky Business project

Elected Members

Councillor Roger Stone	Leader
Councillor Paul Lakin	Deputy Leader
Councillor Caven Vines	
Councillor Ann Russell	
Councillor John Turner	
Councillor John Doyle	

Former Elected Members

Jahangir Akhtar
Brian Cutts
Maurice Kirk
Mark Edgell
Shaun Wright

South Yorkshire Police

Jason Harwin	District Commander
Phil Etheridge	Temporary Detective Superintendent
Matt Fenwick	Detective Superintendent
Claire Mayfield	Temporary Detective Inspector
Dave Walker	Detective Sergeant, Sexual Exploitation Team
Mark Monteiro	Detective Inspector
Malcolm Coe	Temporary Detective Sergeant

Former Police Officers

Christine Davies	District Commander (2001-2005)
Matt Jukes	District Commander (2006-2010)
Richard Tweed	District Commander (2010-2012)
Stephen Parry	Chief Superintendent (2001-02)

Young People

Care leavers group
Youth Cabinet representatives
Focus group of young people
Individual survivors

National Working Group Network

Sheila Taylor MBE	CEO
Bina Parmar	Specialist Team Member
Mike Hand	Specialist Team Member
Ray McMorrow	Specialist Team Member

Others

Steve Ashley	Chair Rotherham Safeguarding Children Board
Professor Pat Cantrill	Author of Serious Case Review Overview Report (Child S)
Saghir Alam	Chair, Rotherham Council of Mosques
Neil Penswick	Ofsted
Gary Smith	Former lay member, the Safeguarding Board
Khalida Luqman	Tassibee Project, Rotherham
Parveen Qureshie	Managing Director, United Multicultural Centre, Rotherham
Mr Abassi	Rotherham Diversity Forum
Azizzum Akhtar	Rotherham Ethnic Minority Alliance
Angie Heal	Author and researcher
Zlakha Ahmed	Chief Executive, Apna Haq
Tracey Haycox	Director of Children and Young People's Services, Safe@Last
Catherine Hall	Lead Nurse, Clinical Commissioning Group
Mark Marriott	Crown Prosecution Service

The Inquiry interviewed several other people who did not wish to be identified, as well as those who contacted the Inquiry's confidential email and Freepost addresses.

Appendix 4: Legal and Policy Context

1. A timeline is set out below demonstrating how policy, statute and guidance have developed in relation to the issue of child sexual exploitation (CSE) over the last two decades. The timeline also refers to criminal prosecutions related to CSE which have been reported in the media within that period. Of significance is the terminology used to describe this social problem, moving from a description of 'child prostitution' to one of 'child sexual exploitation'. This chapter has been largely adapted and updated from the work of Jennifer Moss (2012). The National Working Group Network for Sexually Exploited Children intends to publish the full text on its website, and to keep it updated.

1984

2. **The Child Abduction Act 1984 Section 2** states that it is a criminal offence if a person "without lawful authority or reasonable excuse, takes or detains a child under the age of 16 so as to remove him from the lawful control of any person having lawful control of the child or so as to keep him out of the lawful control of any person entitled to lawful control of the child". It carries a penalty of imprisonment. The Act abolished the crime of 'child stealing' and restricted the offence of kidnapping children. Offenders can be arrested and prosecuted for this Section 2 offence without a complaint from the victim.

3. **Child Abduction Warning Notices** are issued under this legislation in relation to children and young persons who persistently go missing and place themselves at significant risk of harm by forming associations and relationships with inappropriate individuals, sometimes much older than themselves. In so doing they can leave themselves vulnerable, particularly to sexual or physical exploitation. A child/young person may go missing repeatedly and nearly always be found to have been in the company of the same adult, deemed inappropriate to be associating with them. In order to disrupt the criminal or undesirable activities of adults associating with young people, police can serve Child Abduction Warning Notices, formerly known as Harbourers Warning Notices. These Notices tend to be used where arrest/prosecution for any substantive offences is not available or is inappropriate at that time. A Child Abduction Warning Notice identifies the child/young person and confirms that the suspect has no permission to associate with or to contact or communicate with the child. If the suspect continues to do so, they may be arrested and prosecuted for an offence under Section 2 of the Child Abduction Act 1984 or Section 49 of the Children and Young Persons Act 1989.

1994

4. In 1994, **Barnardo's** set up the UK's first child sexual exploitation programme in Bradford. There are now 21 centres nationally, dedicated to turning around the lives of thousands of sexually exploited young people. All this began as a pilot project,

developed into Streets and Lanes working with 'child prostitutes', and is now known as Turnaround. Kay Kelly, who has worked for the Bradford project for 12 years, looks back to her first years with Streets and Lanes: 'The reality wasn't recognised. These young people weren't seen as victims. They were very much seen as perpetrators themselves and treated as adult prostitutes. Of course they weren't, because they were all under the legal age for consent'.

1996

5.   CROP – the **'Coalition for the Removal of Pimping'** - was founded in 1996. This is a child protection charity based in West Yorkshire. It is driven by the experiences and needs of affected parents, and describes itself as the 'only UK organisation to specialise in working alongside the parents, carers and wider family of child sexual exploitation victims'.

1997

6.   One of the first successful CSE criminal prosecutions to be taken was in Leeds in 1997, when two men were convicted, although twenty men were investigated. Since that date there have been over 20 such court cases and a number of men convicted of offences relating to CSE activity.

1998

7.   **The Crime and Disorder Act 1998.** Section 17 of this Act places a duty on a local authority to do all it can do to prevent crime and disorder in its area. Section 17 is aimed at putting crime and disorder reduction at the heart of local decision making; it is a key component in the work of the Safer Communities Partnership, Drug Action Team, Youth Offending Team, the Children's Trust and the Local Safeguarding Children Board (LSCB). Section 115 provides any person with a power but not an obligation to disclose information to responsible public bodies such as the local authority and the Police. The ability to share data does not override safeguards for disclosure of personal data in other legislation or in common law such as defamation, data protection and duties of confidentiality.

8.   **The Data Protection Act 1998.** The Act allows for disclosure without the consent of the data subject in certain conditions, including for the purposes of the prevention or detection of crime, or the apprehension or prosecution of offenders; and where failure to disclose would be likely to prejudice those objectives in a particular case. 'Data' are defined in section 1 of the Act as, inter alia, "Information in a form in which it can be processed by equipment operating automatically in response to instructions given for that purpose".

1999

9. **'Working Together to safeguard children: a guide to inter-agency working to safeguard and promote the welfare of children'** was first published in 1999. This guidance has subsequently been revised in 2006 and 2010 and was reissued in 2012. 'Working Together' sets out how organisations and individuals should work together to safeguard and promote the welfare of children and young people in accordance with the Children Acts 1989 and 2004.

2000

10. Supplementary guidance to 'Working Together' was issued by the Department of Health (which had responsibility for policy on children's services at that time) in May 2000, entitled **'Safeguarding Children Involved in Prostitution'.** This was superseded by new guidance issued by the Department for Education and Skills in 2006.

11. **Multi Agency Public Protection Arrangements** (MAPPA) is the name given to arrangements in England and Wales for the "responsible authorities" tasked with the management of registered sex offenders, violent and other types of sexual offenders, and offenders who pose a serious risk of harm to the public. The "responsible authorities" of the MAPPA include the National Probation Service, HM Prison Service and England and Wales police forces. MAPPA is coordinated and supported nationally by the Public Protection Unit within the National Offender Management Service. MAPPA was introduced by the **Criminal Justice and Courts Services Act 2000** and was strengthened under the **Criminal Justice Act 2003.**

12. MAPPA legislation does not provide the lawful authority for exchanging information on non-MAPPA persons. However, many police forces have taken steps to agree local protocols with partner agencies for providing risk assessment and management of these individuals outside of MAPPA. The **MARAC** process – **Multi Agency Risk Assessment Conference** Process - is part of a coordinated community response to domestic abuse, which aims to:

- share information to increase the safety, health and well-being of victims/survivors – adults and their children;

- determine whether the alleged perpetrator poses a significant risk to any particular individual or to the general community;

- construct jointly and implement a risk management plan that provides professional support to all those at risk and reduces the risk of harm;

- reduce repeat victimisation;

- improve agency accountability; and

- improve support for staff involved in high-risk domestic abuse cases.

13. The focus of the MARAC is the protection of the high-risk victim of domestic abuse. A meeting is convened to share information and enable an effective risk

management plan to be developed. It does not address the issue of intelligence sharing within the CSE risk environment.

2002

14. **'It's someone taking a part of you': a study of young women and sexual exploitation.** Jenny Pearce, Mary Williams, and Cristina Galvin. National Children's Bureau (NCB), 2002.

15. Based on 55 case studies, conducted in partnership with the NSPCC, the study considers the choices and opportunities available to young women who are at risk of, or are experiencing, sexual exploitation. It presents young women's accounts of their experiences, identifies three categories of risk: at risk of sexual exploitation; swapping sex for accommodation, money, drugs or other favours 'in kind'; and selling sex. It recommends interventions that could take place at each stage to support the young women concerned. A summary of this report is available: **'The choice and opportunity project: young women and sexual exploitation'** (PDF).

2000 – 2004

16. In 2000 the death of 8 year old **Victoria Adjo Climbiè** occurred in the London Borough of Haringey. The subsequent Inquiry into Victoria's death was chaired by Lord Laming. The findings of the Inquiry (encapsulated within the **'Laming Report'**) were damning, not only about individual practice failings, poor or non-existent inter-agency working and the lack of focus on the child, Victoria, but also, for the first time, about the failure of senior managers in various organisations to account for the shortcomings of their departments and their resistance, in most cases, to accept responsibility for them. There then followed the 'Every Child Matters' initiative, the introduction of the **Children Act 2004** and the creation of the Office of the Children's Commissioner.

17. **'Every Child Matters; Change for Children'** followed from the Government Green Paper entitled 'Every Child Matters'. The subsequent Children Act was passed in November 2004. For children and young people there are five stated outcomes embedded within this framework that are seen as key to well-being in childhood and later life. These are: being healthy, staying safe, enjoying and achieving, making a positive contribution and achieving economic well-being. These five outcomes constitute the focus of Government attention for all school pupils.

18. **The Children Act 2004** raised the degree of accountability, especially at local authority level. It brought all local government functions of children's welfare and education under the statutory authority of local **Directors of Children's Services**. The Act also required local authorities to appoint a **Lead Member** for children's services, and it placed a statutory duty on authorities to establish **Local Safeguarding Children Boards**. These Boards were given powers to investigate and review inter-agency failings. They have a responsibility to promote the safety

and care of all children and a proactive role to target particular groups of vulnerable children, and by engaging in responsive work to protect children who are suffering, or are likely to suffer significant harm. They co-ordinate the activities of Board members and ensure their effectiveness.

19. In 2002 there was recognition by Staffordshire Police that there was a CSE issue in the Stoke on Trent Policing division and **Operation Sorcerer** was launched. This identified 47 victims of CSE.

20. Following the murder of Holly Wells and Jessica Chapman, an inquiry was set up in 2003 under Sir Michael Bichard. **The Bichard Report** suggested that when assessing under-18s at risk of sexual exploitation professionals should consider the following points in deciding whether to refer to police or children's services:

    - age or power imbalances;

    - coercion, bribery, overt aggression or the misuse of substances as a disinhibitor;

    - whether the child's own behaviour, because of the misuse of substances, places him/her at risk so that he/she is unable to make an informed choice about any activity;

    - whether any attempts to secure secrecy have been made by the sexual partner, beyond what would normally be considered usual in teenage relationships;

    - whether the sexual partner is known to one of the agencies; and

    - whether the child denies, minimises or accepts concerns.

21. In November 2003, a Blackpool teenager, **Charlene Downes**, disappeared. She was believed to have been subject to sexual exploitation. Charlene has never been seen since this time and is believed to have been killed by her abuser/s. A subsequent investigation revealed 'endemic' sexual abuse in the town and the 'Project Awaken' Team was set up as a response. The team brought together professionals from licensing, social services, education and police. It aimed to root out and arrest the abusers before they did serious harm, and to protect children from exploiters. Officers targeted what they called "honey pots", likely to attract both children and offenders, such as takeaways, amusement arcades and the pier, which Charlene visited the night she vanished. The Guardian journalist Julie Bindel wrote in May 2008 'Early on in the investigation, police became aware that Charlene and a number of other girls had been targeted by abusers active in the town. It emerged that the girls had been swapping sex for food, cigarettes and affection. Police are certain that Charlene was sexually abused by one or more men, over a period of time before she went missing, and that her death was linked to the abuse'.

22. In 2012, the trial of two men accused over Charlene's murder was halted when the jury failed to reach a verdict. The subsequent retrial collapsed owing to concerns over a key prosecution witness. Both men were cleared of the charges. The case is

still open.

23. **The Sexual Offences Act 2003** replaced older sexual offences laws with more specific and explicit wording. It also created several new offences such as non-consensual voyeurism, grooming, abuse of position of trust, assault by penetration and causing a child to watch a sexual act. The Act covered offences committed by UK citizens whilst abroad. It also updated and strengthened the monitoring of sex offenders under the Sex Offenders Act 1997.

- sections 47 to 50 prohibit child prostitution;

- sections 52 and 53 prohibit pimping for financial gain; and

- sections 57 to 59 create offences relating to sex trafficking.

24. Prostitution of children or child prostitution is the commercial sexual exploitation of children in which a child performs the services of prostitution, for financial benefit. The term normally refers to prostitution by a minor, or person under the legal age of majority. Human trafficking is the illegal trade of human beings for the purposes of commercial sexual exploitation or forced labour.

25. **'Children and Families: Safer from Sexual Crime'.** The Sexual Offences Act 2003' was published by the Home Office in May 2004.

26. **'Operation Parsonage'** in Keighley, West Yorkshire during 2003, the Police interviewed 33 girls aged between 13 and 17 years. Up to 50 men were believed to have been involved in the exploitation of young girls in the area. Ten men were charged with offences and two convicted.

27. **Lord Laming's report: 'Keeping Children Safe'.** The Government's response to The Victoria Climbiè Inquiry Report and Joint Chief Inspectors' Report Safeguarding Children.' Published in 2003, the report found that many of the reforms brought in after Victoria Climbiè's death in 2000 had not been implemented.

28. In 2004, Anna Hall made a documentary **'Edge of the City'** for Channel 4. It is a film dealing with, among other matters, CSE in Keighley. The film originally started as a documentary about Bradford Social Services Department but became controversial when it highlighted the area's problem of CSE.

29. **'The Lost Teenage'** was a CROP document examining the impact of child sexual exploitation on children and young people as they move into adulthood.

2005

30. **'Work in Progress, Parents, Children and Pimps: Families Speak Out About Sexual Exploitation'** by Aravinda Kosaraju is the title of a further document published by CROP in 2005. This is described as 'A comprehensive research report,

together with parents' personal accounts, which details CROP's work, the demographic profile for families supported by CROP, the nature and impact of sexual grooming and exploitation, and the interventions required to end sexual exploitation.'

31. **'Who are the Victims?'** is a CROP article published in 2005 which 'questions who the victims of sexual exploitation are and the ways in which different channels and agencies can help victims of sexual exploitation.'

32. **'Sexual Exploitation as a Business'** is another documentary from CROP in 2005, described as 'A document analysing the child sexual exploitation processes and the criminal networks involved.'

33. **Intervention orders**, introduced by section 20 of the Drugs Act 2005, can be attached to ASBOs to tackle anti-social behaviour arising from drug misuse. These and other orders may be used in CSE cases where there is also drug or alcohol misuse and anti-social behaviour associated with wider CSE behaviour.

2006

34. In April 2006 there was a prosecution in **Blackpool** for the multiple rape of a 16 year old girl by four men. Two of the men, illegal immigrants, were jailed as a result of the prosecution. The victim and a friend were given alcohol at an Indian restaurant before being taken to an attic and assaulted. One victim said she was abused by four men.

35. The first revision of **'Working Together to Safeguard Children'** occurred in 2006.

36. **'Trafficking in our Midst – Parallels Between International and National Trafficking'** is a 2006 documentary by CROP 'highlighting the parallels between international and national trafficking covering the role of the UK Human Trafficking Centre, legislation, prosecution, organised crime, scale of the problem and responding to the similarities of victim impact.'

2007

37. An **Oldham** CSE case was prosecuted in June 2007. The case concerned the grooming and abuse of 20 girls in the Oldham area. 20 men were arrested and three were charged with rape. Eventually, two convictions for abduction were secured. It was reported in 2011 that since 2007 over 21 Oldham girls had been sexually exploited in incidents of roadside grooming. An Oldham man was convicted in September 2011 for grooming and in April 2012 a case involving 11 men from Oldham and Rochdale came to trial.

38. In August 2007 Peter Connolly known as **'Baby P'** died at the hands of his carers in Haringey London. Peter's death resulted in criminal convictions, two Serious Case Reviews and a further review of safeguarding procedures nationally.

39. In August 2007, following a **Blackburn** CSE court case, two Pakistani nationals aged 46 and 32 were jailed for 7 years and 8 months on charges including abduction, sexual activity with a child and supplying drugs. Girls in the care of social services in Blackburn were targeted and offered to brothers, uncles and friends for sex.

40. Barnardo's published a Pilot Study **'Sexual Exploitation Risk Assessment Framework'** (SERAF) in October 2007.

41. 'Review of Social Services Responses to Safeguarding Children from Sexual Exploitation', a CROP document, was published.

2008

42. In January 2008 a **Sheffield** CSE criminal case saw the conviction of two men for sexual offences against young girls. The court described the relationships as 'exploitative, coercive and possessive.'

43. In a further **Oldham** CSE court case in April 2008, two men were convicted of offences against a 14 year old 'runaway' girl.

44. In October 2008, the Department for Children, Schools and Families (DCSF) published **'Information sharing. Further guidance on legal issues'.** This gives information on the pieces of legislation which may provide statutory agencies and those acting on their behalf with statutory powers to share information. The guidance is for practitioners who have to make decisions about sharing personal information on a case-by-case basis, whether they are working in the public, private or voluntary sectors or providing services to children, young people, adults and/or families. The guidance is also for managers and advisors who support these practitioners in their decision making and for others with responsibility for information governance. It includes:

- the Human Rights Act 1998 and the European Convention of Human Rights;
- common law duty of confidentiality;
- Data Protection Act 1998; and
- specific legislation containing express powers to share information.

45. In November 2008 following a **Manchester** CSE court case, two men were convicted of offences against three vulnerable 15 year-old girls. Also in November 2008 in **Blackburn,** two men were convicted of offences against two 14 year-old girls.

46. In December 2008 the publication of the **Ofsted report into the death of Peter Connolly** resulted in public scrutiny regarding safeguarding practice. This saw increasing numbers of referrals to children's social care; more children becoming the subjects of child protection plans; and a rise in the number of children being taken into local authority care. As a result, professional safeguarding priority was to ensure

that the dangers to younger children at risk of neglect and physical harm were assessed and reduced.

47. **Gathering evidence of the sexual exploitation of children and young_people: a scoping exercise.** Sue Jago and Jenny Pearce, University of Bedfordshire 2008. This reports a study commissioned by the Government to look at the way in which local partnerships (including Local Safeguarding Children Boards and police forces) tackle the sexual exploitation of children and young people through the disruption and prosecution of offenders. It covers the multi-agency approach, the foundation for effective evidence gathering, developing a disruption plan, preparing a prosecution case, and awareness raising, training and guidance.

48. In 2008, The National Working Group Network developed the following **definition** which is utilised in UK Government guidance and policy.

> *'The sexual exploitation of children and young people under 18 involves exploitative situations, contexts and relationships where young people (or a third person or persons) receive 'something' (e.g. food, accommodation, drugs, alcohol, cigarettes, affection, gifts, money) as a result of performing, and/or others performing on them, sexual activities. Child sexual exploitation can occur through the use of technology without the child's immediate recognition, for example by persuading them to post sexual images on the internet/mobile phones with no immediate payment or gain. In all cases, those exploiting the child/young person have power over them by virtue of their age, gender, intellect, physical strength and/or economic or other resources. Violence, coercion and intimidation are common, involvement in exploitative relationships being characterised in the main by the child or young person's limited availability of choice resulting from their social/economic and/or emotional vulnerability'.*

2009

49. In 2009 **Operation Shelter** focused on identifying children missing from care in Stoke on Trent. This investigation identified 20 girls who had been reported missing on 750 occasions and led to **Operation Microphone**. This resulted in the successful conviction of a Stoke on Trent man involved in CSE.

50. In March 2009 **'The Protection of Children in England: A Progress Report'** by Lord Laming was published.

51. April 2009, in **Blackburn,** two men were convicted of offences against a 12 year old girl.

52. The **'Statutory guidance on children who run away and go missing from home or care'** was published in July 2009 by the Department for Children, Schools and Families.

53.   In July 2009, a total of 4 men in **Skipton** were found guilty of 28 sexual offences against a child aged 12-15 years. Three other men were cleared of all charges.

54.   A 21-year old man was convicted in August 2009 of the rape of a boy in what was described as a 'brutal sex attack'. It is understood that he attacked the boy, aged 12, after approaching him in a takeaway in Whalley Range, **Manchester.**

55.   In August 2009 the Government introduced **'Early identification, assessment of needs and intervention – The Common Assessment Framework' (CAF) for children and young people: A guide for practitioners'.**

56.   2009 also saw the publication by the Department for Children, Schools and Families of 'Safeguarding Children and Young People from Sexual Exploitation: Supplementary guidance to Working Together to Safeguard Children'. This guidance provided Local Safeguarding Children Boards and their partners with a framework for developing strategic and frontline responses to child sexual exploitation.

57.   **'Child Sexual Exploitation: a Compendium of Training,'** by Aravinda Kosarju and Dalia Hawley was published by CROP in 2009. This was 'a compendium of available specialist training on child sexual exploitation in England and Wales compiled by CROP as part of the research and development work funded by the Department for Children, Schools and Families. It is based on a six month survey/audit of CSE training conducted during 2008-09.'

58.   In May 2009 the Government published its **Action Plan** to tackle child sexual exploitation.

2010

59.   Project Topsail was set up to assess the 'landscape of child exploitation' in **Staffordshire.**

60.   In February 2010, a **Rochdale** CSE case came to court. A 16 year-old girl agreed to go to a house where she was given whisky and possibly sleeping medication before being raped several times by three members of a gang, two of whom "used a whisky bottle to further degrade her". A fourth man took pictures of the abuse. The victim was later found wandering the streets, dazed.

61.   In June 2010, Tim Loughton MP and Parliamentary Under Secretary of State for Children and Families announced **a review of child protection**, led by Professor Eileen Munro. At the same time he announced that LSCBs would be required to publish Serious Case Review reports unless there were compelling reasons for this not to happen.

62.   In June 2010 a **Nelson** CSE court case involved two men being convicted of offences against three girls.

63. A **'National Picture of Child Sexual Exploitation and Specialist Provisions in the UK'** was published by the National Working Group Network for sexually exploited children and young people.

64. The two **Baby P Serious Case Reviews** of November 2008 and March 2009 were published in 2010 with identifying details removed.

65. During August 2010 a **Rochdale** criminal prosecution heard that an independent school pupil, aged 14, from Rochdale, went missing from home for several days on two occasions. She was spotted in the town centre, groomed and fed a diet of alcohol and drugs before being forced to have sex with numerous Asian men in flats and to work on the streets as a 'prostitute'. She was finally found after she approached a couple in the street in Manchester and asked them for help. Nine Rochdale men were convicted of offences against a child.

66. In September 2010 a **Preston** CSE court case followed **Operation Deter's** investigation of child sexual exploitation involving girls and older men in Preston. Two men groomed two girls aged 13 and 15 for several months after initially pulling up in a car and befriending them.

67. **The Munro Review: Part One: 'A Systems Analysis'** was published in October 2010. This paper outlined the actions which were being taken to improve management, co-ordination and practice. It recognised the problems caused by widespread restructuring and financial cuts. It called for local authorities to have the confidence to develop their own approaches to child protection. A degree of uncertainty and risk must be accepted.

68. In November 2010 a **Rotherham** CSE court case came to trial; five "sexual predators" were convicted of grooming three girls, two aged 13 and one 15, all under children's social care supervision, before using them for sex. The victims were offered gifts, car rides, cigarettes, alcohol and cannabis. Sex took place in cars, bushes and the play area of parks. A mortgage adviser who drove a BMW and owned several properties, promised to treat a 13-year old "like a princess". Another man pulled the hair of a 13-year old and called her a "white bitch" when she tried to reject his attempt to strip her. Eight men were charged and three were cleared of all charges. One victim, aged 13, said: "They used to tell me they loved me and at the time I believed them. I was a little girl."

69. November 2010, a **Derby** court case, in which 9 men were convicted of grooming and abuse in three separate trials. 'Operation Retriever', involving more than 100 police officers, identified 27 victims. 22 were white, three black and two Asian.

70. Derby CSE Serious Case Review Executive Summary was published in November 2010.

71. In January 2011 **'Puppet on a String' The urgent need to cut children free from sexual exploitation'** was published by Barnardo's. This report found that despite new national guidance, in most local authorities child sexual exploitation was not recognised as a mainstream child protection issue. This report called on the Secretary of State for Education to take the lead in ensuring a fundamental shift in policy, practice and service delivery in England.

72. In March 2011 **'Youth Gangs, Sexual Violence and Sexual Exploitation, A Scoping Exercise for The Office of the Children's Commissioner for England'** was published by Professor J. J. Pearce & Professor J. M. Pitts from The University of Bedfordshire Institute for Applied Social Research.

73. May 2011 the **Munro Review of Child Protection. Final Report: 'A Child Centred System'** was published. This set out proposals for reform which were intended to enable professionals to make the best judgements about the help to be given to children, young people and families. It did not, however, explicitly address issues of child sexual exploitation.

74. In June 2011 **'Letting Children be Children – Report of an Independent Review of the commercialisation and sexualisation of childhood'** was published by Reg Bailey. This Review 'aims to assess how children in this country are being pressured to grow up too quickly, and sets out some of the things that businesses and their regulators, as well as Government, can do to minimise the commercialisation and sexualisation of childhood.'

75. **'Out of Mind, Out of Sight; breaking down the barriers to understanding child sexual exploitation'** was published by the Child Exploitation and Online Protection Centres (CEOP) in June 2011.

76. In August 2011, a **Bradford** court case concerned the grooming and abuse of 13-year old Asian girl. August 2011 also saw the trial and sentence of Stephanie Knight and the 'East Lancashire Rape Gang' at **Burnley Crown Court**. Knight was convicted of conspiracy to rape.

77. October 2011, **'What's going on to Safeguard Children and Young People from Sexual Exploitation? How local partnerships respond to child sexual exploitation'** by Sue Jago, with Lorena Arocha, Isabelle Brodie, Margaret Melrose, Jenny Pearce and Camille Warrington, University of Bedfordshire. This research project explored the extent and nature of the response of LSCBs to the 2009 Government guidance on safeguarding children and young people from sexual exploitation. This found that where the guidance had been followed, there were examples of innovative practice to protect and support young people and their families and to investigate and prosecute their abusers. However, the researchers

found that the delivery of that dual approach to child sexual exploitation was far from the norm.

78. In October 2011 the **Children's Commissioner** launched a two-year inquiry into Child Sexual Exploitation in Gangs and Groups.

79. Published in October 2011, **'Safeguarding Children who may have been Trafficked. Practice Guidance'** was guidance updated from the original publication of 2007. It was updated 'to reflect developments such as the introduction in April 2009 of the National Referral Mechanism and the duty on the UK Border Agency to safeguard and promote the welfare of children, which came into force in November 2009'. It delivered a key commitment in the Government's Human Trafficking Strategy, published in July 2011. It was intended to help agencies and their staff safeguard and promote the welfare of children who may have been trafficked. It was supplementary to, and should be used in conjunction with the Government's statutory guidance: Working Together to Safeguard Children.

80. In November 2011, **'Strategy for Policing Prostitution and Sexual Exploitation'** was published by the Association of Chief Police Officers. This report confirmed that: 'In the case of children and young people, the emphasis is always on safeguarding the young person and on the proactive disruption and prosecution of their abusers'.

81. In November 2011 in response to the earlier Barnardo's report, the Department for Education produced **'Tackling Child Sexual Exploitation: National Action Plan'.** This brought together, for the first time, actions by the Government and a range of national and local partners to protect children from CSE. The Action Plan considers sexual exploitation from the perspective of the child. It highlights areas where more needs to be done and sets out specific actions which Government, local agencies and voluntary and community sector partners need to take.

82. These 'actions' include:

- work with the Association of Chief Police Officers, health professional bodies and the Social Work Reform Board to make sure child sexual exploitation is properly covered in training and guidance for frontline professionals;

- LSCBs to prioritise child sexual exploitation and undertake robust risk assessments and map the extent and nature of the problem locally;

- support organisations like Rape Crisis and local sexual assault referral centres to improve services for young victims. The Plan also included measures to raise awareness by improving sex and relationships education in schools and helping parents know what tell-tale signs to look out for;

- the Police, the Crown Prosecution Service, judges and magistrates to support young witnesses and victims, and increase the use of 'special measures' in court to ease the stress and anxiety of criminal proceedings on young people;

- the criminal justice system to come down hard on perpetrators and make sure victims and their families get the right support. The Plan brings together commitments from the Home Office, Ministry of Justice and the Crown Prosecution Service, including:

    o a new sentencing regime, including mandatory life sentences for anyone convicted of a second very serious sexual or violent crime;

    o in group or gang related cases, trial judges should consider how to minimise the trauma for witnesses by considering whether there is need for repeat cross-examination in the witness box.

83. November 2011, the Channel 4 programme **'Britain's Sex Gangs'** focused on CSE in Bradford and London.

84. **'Missing Children and Adults; A Cross Government Strategy'** was published by the Home Office in December 2011. The strategy outlines the three key objectives to provide the right foundations for any effective local strategy to tackle this issue:

- prevention – reducing the number of people who go missing, including prevention strategies, education work and early intervention in cases where children and adults repeatedly go missing;

- protection – reducing the harm to those who go missing, including a tailored, risk-based response and ensuring agencies work together to find and close cases as quickly as possible at a local and national level; and

- provision – providing support and advice to missing persons and families by referring them to agencies promptly and ensuring they understand how and where to access help.

2012

85. In the **Brierfield** child sexual grooming case of January 2012 a sixth man was charged with conspiracy to rape.

86. In May 2012, as a result of the **Operation Span** in Rochdale, 9 men were convicted and jailed. Two men were acquitted. The men at the centre of the trial were from Rochdale and Oldham. Offences ranged from rape, trafficking, conspiracy to engage in sexual activity with a child, sexual assault and sexual activity with a child. This case was the first prosecution in Britain of the offence of Trafficking within the UK for a sexual offence. Sentences ranged from 19 years to 4 years.

87. Also in May 2012, a **Carlisle** CSE criminal case saw a Carlisle takeaway manager jailed for 15 years for attempting to recruit four girls aged between 12 and 16 into prostitution.

88. **"Tackling child sexual exploitation. Helping local authorities to develop**

effective responses" was published in 2012 jointly by Barnardo's and the Local Government Association.

89.   The trial of two men in **Rochdale** involved four victims.

90.   **An Oldham man** was found guilty of the systematic rape of a three-year-old girl over a period of 14 years until she was 17. He was jailed for 19 years as one of nine men involved in the Rochdale sex-ring convicted of conspiracy to engage in sexual activity with a child and trafficking a child within the UK.

91.   Following the verdicts in the Rochdale child sexual exploitation case, the Secretary of State asked the Deputy Children's Commissioner to report to him urgently on emerging findings from her inquiry into **Child sexual exploitation in gangs and groups.** He asked that the report focus particularly on risks facing children living in children's homes. The report was published on 3 July together with the Government's response to its recommendations, which were accepted in full. The action announced by Government also took account of the Joint All Party Parliamentary Groups **(APPG) Report into Children who Go Missing from Care** which was issued on 18 June. The APPG report emphasised the need to tackle failings in arrangements to safeguard children in residential care, and made recommendations similar to those of the Deputy Children's Commissioner.

92.   The Government directed the following immediate action in response:

- making sure there is a clearer picture of how many children go missing from care, and of where they are, by improving the quality and transparency of data;

- ensuring children's homes are properly protected and safely located by removing barriers in regulation, so that Ofsted can share information about the location of children's homes with the Police, and other relevant bodies as appropriate;

- helping children to be located nearer to their local area by establishing a 'task and finish group' to make recommendations by September on strengthening the regulatory framework on out-of-area placements; and

- establishing a further expert working group to look at the quality of children's homes. This would review all aspects of the quality of provision in children's homes, including the management of behaviour and appropriate use of restraint, and the qualifications and skills of the workforce.

93.   In July 2012, the Government published a **Progress report on the implementation of the 'Tackling child sexual exploitation action plan'** and a short step-by-step guide on what frontline practitioners should do if they suspect a child is being sexually exploited.

94.   July 2012, as a result of **Bradford's** criminal investigation into CSE, ten men were

arrested on suspicion of committing serious sexual offences in the area.

95. In August 2012, a CSE criminal case in **Telford** found that four teenage girls had been sexually abused and forced into prostitution by two Shropshire brothers. The jury was told that the youngest girl, 13, was raped, and another was repeatedly sold as a prostitute, sometimes to four men at a time.

96. In September, as a result of Operation Rockferry, **Reading** Crown Court passed sentence on a paedophile ring.

97. In September at **Derby** Crown Court, five men were found guilty of paying for the sexual services of a child; three others admitted the same charge. The men, who acted independently of each other, targeted girls aged between 14-17 in Derby from care homes or difficult backgrounds.

98. On 24th September 2012, **The Times** reported Andrew Norfolk's investigation into CSE in **Rotherham.**

99. In September, a **Rochdale** man was sentenced for the rape of 16-year old girl.

100. In September, as a result of 'Operation Bullfinch' in **Oxford,** nine men were accused of involvement in a child sex-trafficking ring involving six girls over an 8-year period.

2013

101. In March 2013, **'Working Together to Safeguard Children'** was published by the Government. This paper reiterated that the child's needs were paramount and the child's needs and wishes must be put first; that all professionals should share information and discuss any concerns about a child with partner agencies; that initiatives must be based on evidence and available data. The guidance required LSCBs to publish local protocols for assessment and a threshold document specifying the criteria for referral for assessment and the level of early help to be provided. It imposed duties towards safeguarding on a wide range of agencies. LSCBs had to maintain a local learning and improvement framework shared across partner agencies. A national panel of independent experts would advise LSCBs on the initiation and publication of Serious Case Reviews.

102. In June 2013 **The Home Affairs Select Committee report** was published. Its 36 sections endorsed recommendations of earlier papers. Children must be seen as victims, not perpetrators, and the concept of 'consent' must be challenged. There should be widespread training in recognizing signs of grooming and exploitation. Reports and other documents should be in a standard format to facilitate comparisons for scrutiny purposes. The right of redaction should rest with the victim or family or an independent person, not the Safeguarding Children Board.

103. The report recommended improvements to the justice system, the treatment of

victims, the support given to them throughout the judicial process, their cross-examination, the importance of the language used in court, the need for specialist courts with trained judges, prosecutors, ushers.

104.   Accident and Emergency Departments should link more closely with Safeguarding Children Boards in relation to children up to 16 years; likewise sexual health services. The mental health implications of CSE must be recognised in practical measures. The voluntary sector in this field must be adequately funded.

105.   Agencies should acknowledge the suspected model of localised grooming of young white girls by men of Pakistani heritage, instead of being inhibited by the fear of affecting community relations. People must be able to raise concerns without fear of being labelled racist. Offenders' communities should do more to report and tackle the issue. Outreach work towards them is essential. Multi-agency Safeguarding Hubs should be set up, linked to the Crown Prosecution Service.

106.   In October 2013, Ofsted published its **Review of the Local Safeguarding Children Board.** This was a consultation relating to the framework within which future inspections of LSCBs would be conducted by Ofsted.

107.   13 November 2013. The final report from the Office of the Children's Commissioner's Inquiry into **Child Sexual Exploitation in Gangs and Groups** was published. The report criticised services for persistently failing to safeguard children and being in denial about the scale of the issue. It found only 6% of Local Safeguarding Children Boards were complying with key government guidance on tackling CSE. Although it recognised local good practice, the report concluded that there were serious gaps in the knowledge, practice and services required to tackle CSE, despite 'heightened alert'. The report instead proposed a new framework, **'See Me, Hear Me'**, for those who commission, plan or provide protective services. The report was accompanied by two other reports from the Inquiry, which highlighted the risk to young people and the complexities around their understanding of sexual consent.

2014

108.   In February 2014, the Children's Commissioner published 'Sex without consent. I suppose that is rape – how young people understand consent to sex', and in April 'Rights4me', a young person's guide to working together to safeguard children.

109.   In January 2014, the Department of Health published the **'Health Working Group report on child sexual exploitation'.** The report made eleven recommendations covering the identification and treatment of victims; training and e-learning; the co-ordination of services; commitment to multi-agency teams and the role of school nurses.

Appendix 5: Recommendations from earlier reports collated by the Safeguarding Board

1. The RLSCB to review the 2013-16 Business plan and annual plan to produce a more dynamic, user-friendly report for 2013-14.

2. The LSCB to review and refresh the multi-agency CSE procedure.

3. To conduct a multi-agency internal review of structures and governance and produce clear charts detailing roles, responsibilities and lines of accountability.

4. The CSE sub group to review the CSE action plan and ensure it is a practical and useful tool for delivery of strategic actions and its 'actions and milestones' follow SMART principles.

5. RLSCB Chair to provide the opportunity for improved governance and stronger challenge of the CSE action plan at RLSCB meetings

6. A review of the role, membership and future direction of the CSE Sub Group and Silver Group needs to be undertaken.

7. To move the multi-agency CSE Team to a more suitable location.

8. The CSE Team should develop a closer working relationship with the Integrated Youth and Support Service and have specific service pathways in place to support these arrangements.

9. That the role of the CSE Team and its remit and responsibilities need to be reviewed, defined and communicated to all stakeholders.

10. Consideration be given to the appointment or secondment of a senior manager to manage the CSE Team in its entirety and to take the lead role in CSE management in the Borough.

11. A formal tasking and coordinating process should be adopted by the CSE Team.

12. Process mapping needs to be undertaken and CSE pathways developed so that there are clear workflows between the various teams within Children's Social Care, the Early Help Assessment Team and other services in a position to respond to lower level CSE referrals.

13. A needs assessment and mapping exercise should be undertaken in relation to the provision of post-sexual abuse support utilising existing commissioning frameworks.

14. The local authority, as corporate parent for looked after children, to provide the

RLSCB with assurance that Looked After Children and Young People placed out-of-area who go missing receive timely return home interviews which contribute to risk assessments and safety plans.

15. A more formal and SMART performance management system needs to be established under the governance of the Local Safeguarding Children Board.

16. Regular use of Victim / Service User profiling should be utilised to further understand the needs across the Borough and the multi-agency service response that is required.

17. An agreed risk assessment tool, which is fit for purpose, should be developed and implemented as soon as possible.

18. A programme of multi-agency auditing should be introduced in order to evaluate the effectiveness of service provision and outcomes for children and young people at risk of CSE.

19. A longer term training and awareness strategy is required in order to keep the workforce skilled and knowledgeable year on year.

20. The Rotherham Children and Young Persons Improvement Panel under the governance of the RLSCB monitor national reports, inspections and reviews to ensure that where appropriate recommendations from those reports form part of RLSCB processes.

Barnardo's CSE Practice Review

21. We recommend that all key managers and Council members revisit the vision and strategy to establish if the original intentions are effective and delivering the expected changes.

22. A clear media and communication strategy be developed that all agencies and key personnel share and work towards.

23. A named designated manager be identified to manage the day-to-day activities and shape service delivery of the CSE specialist co–located team.

24. In line with the action plan, the positioning of a police analyst within the co-located CSE team.

25. The CSE specialist co-located team to undertake monthly team building and clinical supervision in order to assist in the team's development and understanding of various disciplines and to support the relatively new team in bonding together, understanding each other's roles and developing a shared model of work in practice to meet the needs of sexually exploited young people.

26. The implementation of a South Yorkshire wide CSE Risk Assessment tool.

27. Development of a participation strategy for young people and families involved/ at risk of CSE.

28. It is recommended that the training strategy be widened and adopt a "train the trainer" approach to include **all** faith groups and communities, including the local business community.

29. Annual review of service provision as a way of ensuring that the CSE action plan and CSE strategy are implemented and are effective.

HMIC South Yorkshire Police Response to CSE

(Immediately)

30. The force should review the management of cases by staff in the dedicated child sexual exploitation teams, and ensure this always complies with statutory child protection guidance.

31. The force should communicate and explain to the PCC, staff and other interested parties the delay in deploying the ten additional child sexual exploitation officers to the districts.

32. Failure to fill a vacant post in the Rotherham team that manages sex offenders means that the remaining officers face an unmanageable workload. The force should review the team to ensure that it has sufficient staff to manage sex offenders in line with national guidance.

33. The force should review the staffing arrangements within the Hi-Tech Crime Unit, to ensure these are sufficient to manage effectively the demands of a thorough and comprehensive child sexual exploitation strategy.

34. The force should audit its response to child sexual exploitation, to assess whether the changes it is making are having the desired effect (i.e. of improving outcomes for children), and to identify any further work that is required.

(Within 3 months)

35. The force should review its internal communication regarding child sexual exploitation and ensure that clear, consistent messages are passed to all officers and staff. The messages should ensure that everyone knows which chief officer is the lead on tackling child sexual exploitation.

36. The force should review the tool used to assess the risk of child sexual exploitation to ensure it provides the best possible reflection of the level of risk faced by victims. This could involve additional training for those using the tool, or a change to the

scoring mechanism used to calculate the level of risk.

37.   The force should translate the PCC's strategic priorities into operational delivery on the ground.

38.   The force should review the workloads of all staff within public protection units to ensure they have the capacity to manage effectively the cases they are allocated.

(Within 6 months)

39.   The force should review its training plan to ensure all staff develop and sustain a good understanding of child sexual exploitation.

40.   The force should review the processes in place to respond to child sexual exploitation in all four districts, with a view to creating greater uniformity, and ensuring all areas attain the high standards achieved in the Sheffield district.

41.   The force should review the operation of its local intelligence units to ensure child sexual exploitation is thoroughly supported by an intelligence approach.

42.   The force should review how it could make better use of research and analysis to support strategies to tackle child sexual exploitation.

43.   The force should review how it monitors the internet for evidence of child sexual exploitation to ensure intelligence opportunities are not being overlooked.

44.   The force and its partners should examine how it can more efficiently manage the handling of child sexual exploitation information and intelligence. In particular, the difficulties in sharing information within the multi-agency teams at Doncaster and Rotherham (because of incompatible information and intelligence IT systems) should be resolved.

"If only someone had listened" – Office of Children's Commissioner

45.   The Department for Education should review and where necessary, revise the *Working Together guidance on CSE* (DCSF, 2009). This should include a review of the definition of CSE.

46.   Every Local Safeguarding Children Board should take all necessary steps to ensure they are fully compliant with the current *Working Together guidance on CSE* (DCSF, 2009).

47.   Every Local Safeguarding Children Board should review their strategic and operational plans and procedures against the seven principles, nine foundations and **See Me, Hear Me** Framework in this report, ensuring they are meeting their obligations to children and young people and the professionals who work with them. Gaps should be identified and plans developed for delivering effective practice in

accordance with the evidence. The effectiveness of plans, procedures and practice should be subject to an ongoing evaluation and review cycle.

48. There need to be nationally and locally agreed information-sharing protocols that specify every agency's and professional's responsibilities and duties for sharing information about children who are or may be in need of protection. At the national level, this should be led and coordinated by the Home Office through the Sexual Violence Against Children and Vulnerable People National Group. At the local level, this must be led by LSCBs. All member agencies at both levels must be signatories and compliance rigorously monitored.

49. Problem profiling of victims, offenders, gangs, gang-associated girls, high-risk businesses and neighbourhoods and other relevant factors must take place at both national and local levels. The Home Office, through the Sexual Violence Against Children and Vulnerable People National Group, should lead and coordinate the development of a national profile. Local Safeguarding Children Boards should do the equivalent at the local level.

50. Every local authority must ensure that its Joint Strategic Needs Assessment includes evidence about the prevalence of CSE, identification and needs of high-risk groups, local gangs, their membership and associated females. This should determine commissioning decisions and priorities.

51. Relationships and sex education must be provided by trained practitioners in every educational setting for all children. This must be part of a holistic/whole-school approach to child protection that includes internet safety and all forms of bullying and harassment and the getting and giving of consent.

52. Through the Sexual Violence against Children and Vulnerable People National Group, the Government should undertake a review of the various initiatives being funded by the Home Office, Department for Education, Department of Health and any others as relevant, in order to ensure services are not duplicated and that programmes are complementary, coordinated and adequately funded. All initiatives should be cross-checked to ensure that they are effectively linked into child protection procedures and local safeguarding arrangements.

www.ingramcontent.com/pod-product-compliance
Lightning Source LLC
Chambersburg PA
CBHW080044280326
41935CB00014B/1783